William Baziotes. *Paintings and Drawings, 1934–1962*

To William Baziotes and his brothers
        Rembrandt — "that magician of magicians"
        Leonardo — "one of the great theoreticians of art"
        Baudelaire — "I was given mud — and I left Gold"
To Ethel Baziotes
        Teacher, dreamer, muse…
        And the best cornerman in the business.

Michael Preble

William Baziotes
Paintings and Drawings, 1934–1962

Curated by
Michael Preble

SKIRA

Cover
The Parachutists, detail, 1944
Duco enamel on canvas, 30 × 40 in
(76,2 × 101,6 cm)
(cat. no. 15)

Back cover
Green Night, 1957
Oil on canvas, 36 1/8 × 48 1/8 in
(91.76 × 122.24 cm)
(cat. no. 45)

Design
Marcello Francone

Editorial Coordination
Franco Ambrosio

Editing
Emma Cavazzini

Layout
Veronica Bellotti

Picture Research
Chiara Barbieri
Sandra Divari

First published in Italy in 2004 by
Skira Editore S.p.A.
Palazzo Casati Stampa
via Torino 61
20123 Milano
Italy
www.skira.net

ISBN 88-7624-051-9

Distributed in North America by Rizzoli
International Publications, Inc., 300 Park
Avenue South, New York, NY 10010.
Distributed elsewhere in the world by
Thames and Hudson Ltd., 181a High
Holborn, London WC1V 7QX, United
Kingdom.

William Baziotes
Paintings and Drawings, 1934–1962

Peggy Guggenheim Collection, Venice
September 5, 2004 – January 9, 2005

Lenders

Doreen and Gilbert Bassin
Constance and David Clapp, New York
Dr. Joseph Cunningham and Dr. Bruce Barnes
Dr. and Mrs. Jerome Dersh
The Helman Collection
Paul Francis and Titia Hulst
Mr. and Mrs. Meredith Long
Elliot K. Wolk
Other private collectors

Jack S. Blanton Museum of Art, The University of Texas
   at Austin
The Baltimore Museum of Art
Birmingham Museum of Art, Alabama
The Cleveland Museum of Art
The Detroit Institute of Arts
Kresge Art Museum, Michigan State University, East
   Lansing, Michigan
Herbert F. Johnson Museum of Art, Cornell University,
   Ithaca, New York
The Minneapolis Institute of Arts
New Orleans Museum of Art
Estate of William Baziotes, New York
Richard L. Feigen & Co., New York
Joseph Helman Gallery, New York
Michael Rosenfeld Gallery, New York
Solomon R. Guggenheim Museum, New York
The Metropolitan Museum of Art, New York
Whitney Museum of American Art, New York
Carnegie Museum of Art, Pittsburgh
Francis Lehman Loeb Art Center, Vassar College,
   Poughkeepsie, New York
Washington University Gallery of Art, St. Louis
Tel Aviv Museum of Art
Krannert Art Museum and Kinkead Pavilion, University
   of Illinois, Urbana-Champaign
Peggy Guggenheim Collection, Venice
Hirshhorn Museum and Sculpture Garden, Smithsonian
   Institution, Washington, D.C.
National Gallery of Art, Washington, D.C.
Smithsonian American Art Museum, Washington, D.C.

The story of how Peggy Guggenheim encouraged the youthful William Baziotes in the early 1940s is told in this catalogue. Sixty years have passed since she gave him his first one-man exhibition, at Art of This Century, New York. He is an artist to whom the history of art has still to do full justice, perhaps because his contemplative and lyrical muse sets his work apart from the gestural, expressionist images of his fellow New York School 'Irascibles' — images that so captured the international imagination in the post-war period. Nevertheless Baziotes was a front rank avantguardist when his youthful work was shown in Breton's and Duchamp's "First Papers of Surrealism" exhibition in 1942. He died much too young, at the height of his powers, aged 50.

In 1965 Lawrence Alloway was charged by Thomas Messer, then director of the Solomon R. Guggenheim Museum, with curating a memorial exhibition for Baziotes. In 2000 Diane Waldman, former deputy director of the Guggenheim, proposed that the Peggy Guggenheim Collection present an exhibition of his paintings and drawings that she was curating for The Butler Institute of American Art, Youngstown, Ohio. This set things in motion. Four years later, with the full support of Joseph Helman, whose gallery represents the Baziotes Estate, and of Ethel, William Baziotes' widow, with Michael Preble (who has embarked on the Baziotes catalogue raisonné) as curator, the Solomon R. Guggenheim Foundation is proud to present what I believe to be the largest retrospective of Baziotes' paintings and drawings ever assembled.

I am very grateful indeed to Ethel Baziotes. Without her consent we would not have proceeded. With her blessing, we have obtained superb loans from museums and private collectors that have assured for us almost without exception Baziotes' finest works. More: in what amounts to a homage to Peggy Guggenheim, Ethel Baziotes has given an important early oil painting, The Parachutists (1944), to the Peggy Guggenheim Collection. It is historically appropriate that this was shown, like several others in this catalogue, at Baziotes' first exhibition, at Art of This Century; but even more gratifying than this is that it enables Baziotes' to be represented permanently in the Guggenheim's Venetian museum which was formerly Peggy Guggenheim's home. Peggy retained two works on paper for her own collection, while the Solomon R. Guggenheim Museum in New York owns beautiful paintings, but only relatively late ones. The Parachutists dispels therefore a lacuna in the representation of Abstract Expressionism in the Guggenheim Foundation as a whole. Mrs Baziotes accompanied her gift with two quotations: from Peggy Guggenheim, "There is method in my madness," and from Sir Joshua Reynolds, "Present and Future — may be considered rivals. He who solicits the one may expect to be discountenanced by the other." The latter surely refers to the dedication, integrity, even an element of self-sacrifice, of the life of William Baziotes.

Joseph Helman is a great friend to the Peggy Guggenheim Collection, and I am especially grateful to him, to Peter Ryan and to Peter Cross, gallery director, who have placed all possible trust, information and expertise at the disposal of Michael Preble as he worked to bring the exhibition about. Michael Preble's professionalism has been a very important asset to the exhibition. Thank you particularly to the long list of those who have let paintings and drawings temporarily leave their walls, whether in museums or homes, to share in this testimony of the grandeur of their maker. It has been a pleasure as on previous occasions to work with Skira, with Massimo Vitta Zelman and Stefano Piantini as well as the Studio Ambrosio, on the publication of this catalogue. Thank you to all the staff of the Peggy Guggenheim Collection who have worked hard to bring about this tribute — its loans, its installation, its catalogue, its marketing, its publicity and opening events, its financial administration, its day-to-day operation and safeguarding, and the retailing which will enable visitors to carry away an enduring memory of a won-derful artist. I draw your attention to the list of this small, hard-working staff at the back of this catalogue. In the same place you will find the lists of our Advisory Board members, of our Institutional Patrons and of In-trapresae Collezione Guggenheim. Their combined generosity makes possible what we do.

Thomas Krens
Director, The Solomon R. Guggenheim Foundation

First and foremost, I wish to acknowledge with deepest gratitude the support and encouragement of Ethel Baziotes. Since my first contact with her in 1971, as an intern at the National Collection of Fine Arts, to our most recent telephone conversation, Ethel has been a source of information and insight. But most importantly, she continually provides me with inspiration — she has been my muse — in guiding my devotion to her husband's work.

To the many museum directors and curators who supported loans to the exhibition, I am exceedingly grateful. With some thirty years of museum experience, I appreciate the hours that directors, curators, registrars, preparators and others contribute to making such an effort a success.

A special thanks is also extended to the private collectors, whose own courage and devotion led them to acquire a Baziotes. Knowing the special bond that exists with the work, I am grateful for their willingness to part with it for the exhibition.

In New York, I wish to thank Joseph Helman, Joseph Helman Gallery, for his devotion to the work and his support of my endeavors. I also appreciate the extra attention provided by Peter Cross, Joseph Helman Gallery; Peter Ryan; Susan Davidson, Curator at the Solomon R. Guggenheim Museum; Michael Rosenfeld at Michael Rosenfeld Gallery; Richard Feigen of Richard L. Feigen & Co.; and the museum services departments of Sotheby's and Christie's, in particular Lauren Shadford of Sotheby's an Allison Whiting of Christie's. For their assistance in gathering photographs of the artist, I wish to thank Arnold Newman, Roberta Lazarus, and David Heald of the Solomon R. Guggenheim Museum. The exceptional enthusiasm of Joseph Cunningham and Bruce Barnes is also acknowledged. I am grateful to Charles Seliger for his insightful contribution.

In Reading, Pennsylvania, I am grateful for the research assistance of Kathy M. Scogna; Joe Reddy, Reading Eagle; George M. Meiser, President, Historical Society of Berks County; and Vasti F. DeEsch, Reading Public Museum.

In Washington, D.C., thanks to Wendy Hurlock at the Archives of American Art, for her assistance in gathering archival and photographic materials.

In Little Rock, Arkansas, I wish to thank Missy Wright Anderson for her editing of the text — her dedication to language is exemplary; and Patrice O'Donoghue, Li-

brarian at the Arkansas Arts Center's Taylor Library, for her research assistance.

In Norfolk, Virginia, thanks to Mary Anne Vandivort, Kirn Memorial Library, City of Norfolk, for her interlibrary loan expertise; and to the dedicated core of volunteers at the Jean Outland Chrysler Library of the Chrysler Museum of Art, who helped me utilize this extraordinary resource.

The patience of my wife, Anne Guthrie, should not go unrecognized.

Finally, my gratitude is extended to the Peggy Guggenheim Collection. The value of Director Philip Rylands' invitation to participate and his ongoing confidence cannot be measured. Two members of his staff have worked beyond the call of duty: Jasper Sharp, Exhibitions and Collections Coordinator, who in working out all of the many components of this project made the distance between Norfolk and Venice feel like a mere traghetto ride across the Grand Canal; and Chiara Barbieri, Manager of Publications, who single-handedly coordinated the two-language catalogue and all other exhibition printed matter. The Peggy Guggenheim Collection staff is a joy to work with, and I want also to thank the many others who in their different roles have created and managed the whole apparatus of researching, gathering, installing, opening, marketing, communicating, safeguarding and operating a complex loan exhibition such as this.

Michael Preble
Curator

William Baziotes: Passages

Michael Preble

A Classicist in New York

When William Baziotes moved from Reading, Pennsylvania, to New York City in August 1933, he encountered a vibrant city. In the visual arts, New York was about to experience a transformation that would propel it well past Paris as the center of the art world.

It is likely that every artist, new to New York and ready to make a mark, would seek out the beacons of modernism and the avant-garde. In Manhattan, these sources were the Museum of Modern Art, founded in 1929; the Whitney Museum of American Art, in 1930; the Solomon R. Guggenheim Museum, in 1939; and the Museum of Living Art, in 1927. Each began to build its reputation quickly with acquisitions and remarkable exhibitions. In the early 1930s the Museum of Modern Art showed German Expressionism, Diego Rivera's murals and French-inspired modernist work.[1] The years 1936 to 1939 at the same museum were distinguished by a series of history-making exhibitions — first the vanguard "Cubism and Abstract Art," followed in 1937 by the influential "Fantastic Art: Dada and Surrealism," in 1939 by the breakthrough Picasso exhibition, and in 1941 by an important Miró retrospective.

Just forty blocks to the south, the Whitney Museum of American Art was seeking its own distinct character. In contrast to the international and historical styles of the Museum of Modern Art, the Whitney seemed downright homey, very American, and, reflecting its Greenwich Village confines, very welcoming to the egalitarian, bohemian neighborhoods that surrounded it. The Whitney set the tone for its support of American-Scene painting and social realism right from the start. Its inaugural exhibition included Edward Hopper's *Early Sunday Morning*, Reginald Marsh's *Why Not Use the 'L'?*, John Steuart Curry's *Baptism in Kansas*, Guy Pène du Bois' *Woman With a Cigarette* and, giving a nod to modernism, Stuart Davis' *Place Pas de Loup* and Charles Demuth's *My Egypt*.

The Solomon R. Guggenheim Museum opened its doors in 1939 as the Museum of Non-Objective Painting in a former automobile showroom on East 54th Street. In its fostering of recent European art, it became a showcase for such artists as Vasily Kandinsky, Paul Klee and Piet Mondrian. Some twenty years later, it entered a new era as it moved into Frank Lloyd Wright's architectural landmark on Fifth Avenue.

Another source for avant-garde European art was the Museum of Living Art, the collection gathered by the successful banker Albert E. Gallatin that was housed at New York University from 1927 to 1943. It included work by Cézanne, Picasso, Braque, Gris, Léger, Arp, Miró and Masson, as well as paintings by many Neoplasticist and Constructivist artists. The collection was a popular venue for American artists and students who were interested in Cubism and abstraction.

Baziotes, however, fresh from the comforts of family life in south-eastern Pennsylvania, was not yet ready to participate in museum exhibitions. There was still much learning ahead.

Born Vasillios Angelus Baziotes in 1912 in Pittsburgh, William Baziotes was the son of Stella and Frank Angelus Baziotes. His father had arrived in America from Greece in 1896. In 1911 he returned to his homeland, where a matchmaker brought him together with Stella Eliopoulos, a cheese vendor's daughter. In an interview with Donald Paneth in 1952, Baziotes recalled that his father's family had been known as violinists in their village, and his grandfather was a shepherd.[2] In 1913 the family moved to Reading for business opportunities. Baziotes remarked to Paneth that his father was a dedicated family man with a strong work ethic — ambitious with strict business standards. His early memories were those of an active, playful child, who for a time enjoyed the benefits of middle-class life.

Baziotes would soon experience another side of life. When his father's successful restaurant burned in 1919, the loss of income forced the family into far more modest quarters. His new neighborhood was Reading's equivalent to New York's Bowery, where honky-tonks, bars, brothels, pawnshops and a new cast of characters, gamblers and gangsters alike, prowled the streets. As the family fortunes improved through a series of endeavors, including a successful lunch room and wholesale bakery, the adolescent Baziotes became more rambunctious, frequenting the vaudeville and burlesque shows along 7th Street. It was during this period that he developed a life-long fondness for boxing; for a time he even considered boxing professionally.

Unexpectedly, his desire to live his life as an artist became increasingly important. His tentative drawing efforts in high school were recognized and praised by teachers, but he was no prodigy. He did have skill and a strong will. After a brief stint as an office boy in the advertising department of the *Reading Times*, he found new inspiration at J. M. Kase & Company, a stained glass manufacturer. There, from 1931 to 1933, his job of antiquing glass proved to be an excellent foundation for exploring the qualities of line, color and light.

At this time he befriended the poet Byron Vazakas, who encouraged the nascent artist to seek more worthwhile endeavors, away from Reading. And then it came to him:

"I told my father, 'I think I ought to go to New York.' He said, 'No, wait till I make some money and you can go in style.' Now I felt even more depressed. I stuck around town through June, but I felt I was prolonging something. I knew I wanted to get out."[3]

Baziotes left Reading for New York in August 1933. "Art came in like a growth, bothering me," he says. "It wasn't really a choice, but kind of like fate, I had to do it."[4] Throughout his life, Reading would remain important. He would visit his family every summer with his wife Ethel and spend time painting, relaxing and enjoying the countryside. Ethel Baziotes' described these sojourns as "Bill's umbilical cord, reminding him where he came from."

Once in New York, Baziotes enrolled at the National Academy of Design. There he studied well into 1936 with Charles Curran, Ivan Olinsky, Gifford Beal and Leon Kroll. His sketchbooks from the period, two of which are in the National Gallery of Art in Washington, D.C., are filled with the kind of observations that Edgar Degas might have made in New York — simple moments, quiet scenes on a park bench or at a neighborhood eatery, and the occasional nude study, probably assignments from Leon Kroll's figure drawing class (fig. 1). However, the genteel American impressionism and picturesque realism of his teachers had a limited effect on the young artist.

Instead, Baziotes' inspirations were the old masters in the galleries of the Metropolitan Museum of Art — Piero della Francesca, Titian, Rembrandt, Rubens, Velázquez, Goya, Fragonard, Ingres and Corot.[5] Ethel Baziotes recalled in a recent interview that these sources continued to influence him in later life. "Every day they are my conscience," he frequently said. Earlier, he also visited the Museum of Natural History; its specimens and exhibits were to be inspirational for future iconography. Yet so much more was on the horizon, for Baziotes was about to confront the challenges of Surrealism and Cubism.

Europe Comes Ashore

Baziotes never traveled to Europe, so he did not see the seminal exhibition of Surrealist objects in Paris

1
William Baziotes,
Page from a
Sketchbook, 1930s
Washington, D.C.,
National Gallery
of Art, Gift of
Mr and Mrs Robert
Harris

nor the historic "International Surrealist Exhibition" at the New Burlington Gallery, London, both held in 1936. There is no documentation that Baziotes saw the pioneering 1937 "Dada and Surrealism" exhibition at the Museum of Modern Art, but he probably did. He was already familiar with the museum, having visited the Henri Matisse exhibition in 1931.

European Surrealism was not unknown in New York in the 1930s, particularly in the smaller galleries.[6] Between 1933 and 1935, Salvador Dalí, Joan Miró, André Masson, Alberto Giacometti and Jean Arp had exhibitions at the Pierre Matisse, Julien Levy and John Becker galleries. The Surrealist journal *Minotaure*, first published in 1933, documented these exciting new ideas.[7]

And there was the arrival of the artists themselves. Many Dadaists and Constructivists were already in America at the end of the 1930s, including Marcel Duchamp, Amédée Ozenfant, László Moholy-Nagy, Jean Hélion, Josef Albers and Hans Hofmann. As the Germans threatened Paris in 1940, many Parisian artists, including many Surrealists, made their way to America, including André Breton, Marc Chagall, Salvador Dalí, Max Ernst, André Masson, Roberto Matta, Piet Mondrian, Kurt Seligmann, Yves Tanguy and Pavel Tchelitchew.[8]

Baziotes' semi-Surrealist works of this period were elaborations of the superficial characteristics of the movement, and fell short of the fully synthesized Surrealism of his mature work. Nevertheless, Baziotes was departing stylistically and conceptually from his teachers at the National Academy of Design, moving away from traditional academic lessons to an experimentation that would influence his early work.

In the untitled drawings executed between 1934 to 1938 (cat. nos. 1-2), Baziotes relied heavily on familiar Surrealist iconography. The exaggeration of barely recognizable anatomical forms, the contorted violence of bird-animal configurations, the ethereal landscape settings and the more whimsical use of spider shapes and concentric circles all owe some debt to Arp and Dalí. Miró's imagery in the 1920s, such as *Dutch Interior II*, 1928 (fig. 2), and Masson's works of the 1940s and early-1950s, with their aggressive lines and distortions (*Meditation on an Oak Leaf* of 1942 for example, fig. 3), were if anything even stronger influences on the young Baziotes.[9]

To Baziotes' credit, he was determined to come to an understanding of Surrealism by redefining it for himself. He chose two contradictory ways to achieve this — seeking freedom by adopting automatism and then adding structure by assimilating Cubism.

As André Breton, the autocratic keeper of the Surrealist flame, would have it, automatism was a "pure exercise of free association." His definition of the term appears in his *Manifesto of Surrealism*:

"Pure psychic automatism, by which one seeks to express, be it verbally, in writing, or in any other manner, the real working of the mind. Dictated by the unconscious, in the absence of any control exercised by reason, and free from aesthetic or moral preoccupations."[10]

The usefulness of automatism to painters was limited: not only had they consciously to choose their medium and color but they also had to find a means to individual expression. Recognizing that strict adherence to Breton's automatism would produce only chaos, painters reconceived it as chance. By allowing chance or the accidental to occur on canvas — the uncontrolled drip and flow of paint, the overdrawn contour — artists challenged accepted aesthetic traditions and developed their imagery more from their subconscious than their conscious mind.

Individual artists, including the European Surrealists and Surrealist-inspired American artists, found their own unique approaches to automatism in their picture-making processes.[11] For Baziotes and his friends, automatism was clearly an important technique.

In 1940 Baziotes met Matta, and the two remained friends until Matta returned to Europe in 1948; he also met Gordon Onslow Ford and Jimmy Ernst that same year. Matta then introduced Baziotes to Robert Motherwell, who became a good friend. In 1942, Matta, Motherwell and Baziotes, along with Jackson Pollock, Peter Busa and Gerome Kamrowski met at Matta's home, usually on Saturdays, for experiments and critiques in automatism.[12]

In the early 1940s, Baziotes' ink and watercolor drawings (cat. no. 8) develop a newfound spontaneity. The small untitled gouache on paper (cat. no. 4), with its vigorous lack of traditional control, is likely the product, in spirit at least, of the Saturday sessions in automatism. Line-work takes on a more decorative accent in *Night Figure No. 1* (circa 1945; cat. no. 19) while enhancing the contours of the forms and adding a subtle depth to the ground.

A similar treatment of line appears in a later oil painting, *The Web* of 1946 (cat. no. 20).

Baziotes quickly combined this freedom of line with his vocabulary of Surrealist imagery. In *The Accordion of Flesh*, circa 1941 (cat. no. 5), for example, a torso-like image in the center appears confined by a tangled web in a yellow box, while an anthropomorphic figure to the right stretches its tentacular limbs across the picture plane to a totem-like life source on the left.

Baziotes' painting *Leonardo da Vinci's Butterfly*, 1942 (cat. no. 6), is filled with rapid strokes of paint that emanate from several winged shapes like rays of light from a shining prism. Knowing da Vinci's fable, "The Butterfly and the Light," Baziotes envisioned the fragile wings consumed by the picture's inner illumination.[13] This was one of his earliest treatments of the theme of metamorphosis. The work's texture and fantastic topography are reminiscent of Max Ernst's texture studies and Matta's imaginative landscapes (fig. 4). Recalling his early training in Reading, the radiant blues, reds and yellows have the glittering vibrancy of stained glass. Recognizing its value, André Breton and Marcel Duchamp chose the work for inclusion in the "First Papers of Surrealism" exhibition held at the Whitelaw-Reid Mansion in New York in 1942; it was also included in Baziotes' 1944 exhibition at Art of This Century.

Baziotes was not the first to consider automatism as a point of departure rather than an end in itself. This attitude was shared by Max Ernst in his exploitation of the possibilities of *frottage*, by Dominguez' who experimented with *decalcomania*, and by Jean Arp whose random paper cuttings were the source of many of his collages between 1916 and 1930.[14]

It was during this time, from fall 1936 to December 1941, that Baziotes taught under President Roosevelt's innovative Works Progress Administration in both the Federal Art Project and the Easel Painting Project. It offered a regular though modest stipend. In letters to his brother Christopher in Reading, he often recounted in disgruntled terms the delays and difficulties in receiving his funds from the agency.[15]

While continuing his effort to redefine Surrealism in the 1940s, Baziotes embraced Cubism, though with a short-lived admiration. As he did with Surrealism, he carefully chose his favorite elements. The Cubism he chose — for there were many cubistic styles — came from Picasso and Braque's work of 1908 to 1913. Here, Baziotes found simplicity to be inspiring — figures and objects alike were reconfigured into a series of faceted shapes. Though each shape held no independent value, the organized whole evoked a variety of responses — the image seen from several points of view, its physical movement, the passage of time and a gentle play of potential psychological implications. The artist was years away from being influenced by the work of Jung and Freud or from interest in metamorphosis and symbolism.

The Cubist-inspired compositions of Baziotes date from the mid-1940s, and include *The Schoolroom*, 1943 (cat. no. 11); *Three Doors*, 1944 (cat. no. 12); *The Stage*, 1944 (cat. no. 13); *The Wine Glass*, 1944 (cat. no. 14); *The Parachutists*, 1944 (cat. no. 15); *The Hourglass*, circa 1944 (cat. no. 16); *The Room*, 1945 (cat. no. 17); and *Still Life*, 1945 (cat. no. 18). In each, an essential motif — such as the parachute, the wine glass — is exploited for its formal possibilities in the composition.

In *The Parachutists*, the parachute's dome is twisted, turned and inverted; the conical shapes of the cords form a distinct, semi-transparent pattern scattered across the surface. A grid of thick black lines replaces the subtle faceting of Picasso and Braque's Cubism. In *The Room*, he uses recognizable parts of a fan, clock and lamp for their dynamic design qualities. *Three Doors* is the least Cubist of the group; its anthropomorphic figures, set in a stylized totemic arrangement, relate more to his biomorphic images of the late-1940s and early-1950s paintings.

Two paintings clearly show evidence of his earlier job at J. M. Kase & Company in Reading, where he worked on church windows and also stained the glass. In the brilliantly colored *Still Life*, vibrant reds and greens unmistakably look like stained glass panels. In *The Balcony*, 1944 (fig. 5), the shifting tonalities of subdued color, combined with the sensuous flow of line, create a subtly erotic abstract display. The work relates less to Baudelaire's poem or to Matisse's famous painting of the same name than to the power of his experiences with stained glass to impart a love of line and color to the young painter.

2
Joan Miró
Dutch Interior II,
Summer 1928
Oil on canvas,
36 1/4 x 28 3/4 in
Venice, Peggy
Guggenheim
Collection

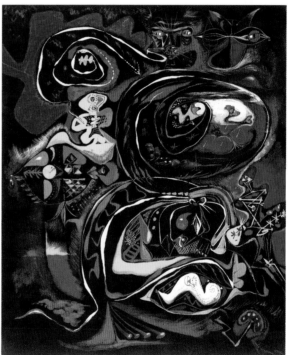

3
André Masson
Meditation on an Oak Leaf, 1942
Tempera, pastel and sand on canvas, 40 x 33 in
New York, The Museum of Modern Art. Given anonymously 1950

4
Matta
Rocks, 1940
Oil on canvas,
38 1/8 x 60 1/8 in
The Baltimore
Museum of Art.
Bequest of Saidie
A. May (BMA
1951.3335)

For gallery owner, entrepreneur and friend Peggy Guggenheim, these canvases had spirit, and her support became invaluable. Through her Art of This Century gallery, Baziotes, Jackson Pollock, Robert Motherwell, David Hare, Charles Seliger and other artists of the burgeoning avant-garde received their first significant public exposure and were eventually celebrated as initiators of a new era of painting.

In April 1943, six months after the opening of the gallery, Baziotes exhibited *The Drugged Balloonist* (cat. no. 9) in a collage exhibition. The work, created with Motherwell's encouragement, contained several shapes cut from magazines and newspapers, including the picture of a propeller. Baziotes did not find the work sufficiently sensuous and did not share Motherwell's enthusiasm for collage as "endlessly pleasurable, fascinating, relaxing and evocative."[16] He also showed in Art of This Century Gallery's "Spring Salon for Young Artists," (*The Mirror at Midnight I and II*, circa 1942; cat. no. 7).

Baziotes' first one-man exhibition was held at Art of This Century in 1944 and included *The Classroom, Three Doors, The Stage, The Parachutists, The Wine Glass* and *The Hourglass.* An anecdote from Baziotes' friend and fellow artist, Robert Motherwell, vividly recalls the fears they all shared:

"I hung Baziotes' show with him at Peggy's in 1944. After it was up and we had stood in silence looking at it for a while, I noticed he had turned white. When he was anxiety-ridden, a white mucus would form around his mouth — his throat must have become very dry with emotion. Suddenly, he looked at me and said, 'You're the one I trust; if you tell me the show is no good, I'll take it right down and cancel it.' At that moment I had no idea whether it was good or not — it seemed so far out; and I reassured him that it was — there was nothing else I could do [...] You see, at the opposite side of the coin of the abstract expressionists' ambition and of our not giving a damn, was also not knowing whether our pictures were even pictures, let alone whether they were any good..."[17]

The gallery experience, which offered the opportunity of sales and the camaraderie of fellow artists, eventually gave him the confidence he needed and put him on the path to success (see the essay of Jasper Sharp in this catalogue).

A Very Good Year

For Baziotes, 1947 was a breakthrough year. He was now ready to win his reputation among the Abstract

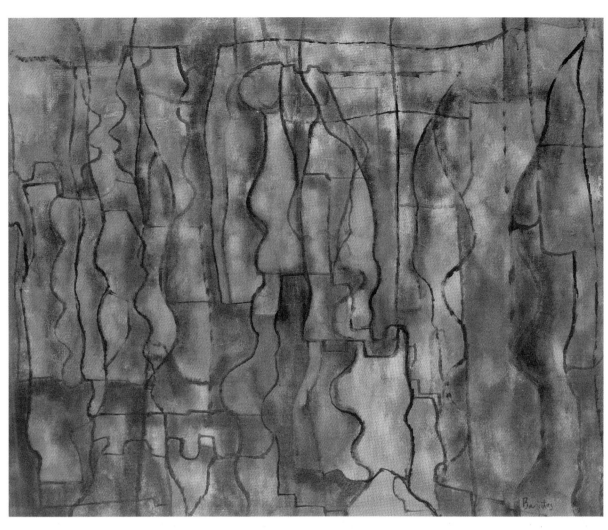

Expressionists as a painter of organic abstractions, imaginary landscapes and mysterious confrontations of a primordial nature. In several key works, Baziotes shows the beginnings of his mature work — the assimilation of the lessons of Surrealism and Cubism — and the development of an iconography and technique that was uniquely his own and distinct from the gestural efforts of his fellow painters.

A small group of important paintings dated 1947 — *Dwarf, Cyclops* and *Night Form* — depicts a single dominant figure in the center of the composition. Articulated within the figure are other curvilinear lines and shapes, as well as familiar images from drawings of the late 1930s, like concentric circles and jagged teeth. These works are characterized by agitated brushwork and are important as the beginning of a personal symbolism.

Dwarf (fig. 6), which was purchased by the Museum of Modern Art, is the most complicated and well-documented of the three. In correspondence dated 26 April 1949 to Alfred H. Barr, Jr., the Mu-

seum of Modern Art's director, Baziotes discussed the painting's inspirations and content.[18] He expressed a fascination with the torso-like figure, whose deformities he attributed to either a human or animal form. His recollection for the source of this horrific image was a book of World War I photographs; he said that one photograph in particular, of a soldier truncated at the waist and without arms, haunted him. (Other sources would have included Pre-Columbian art at the Museum of Natural History and ancient Roman sculpture at the Metropolitan Museum of Art.) The resulting image has neither the playful whimsy of Miró nor the primitivism of Jean Dubuffet's *art brut*, but relates rather to the aggressively drawn figurative abstractions by his friend André Masson from the 1940s and 1950s.

Baziotes further explained to Barr that the teeth were inspired by a crocodile at the Bronx Zoo; the eye from a lizard; and that the lower oval shape was suggestive of the female vagina. The concentric circles reminded him of targets, recalling a frequent im-

age from his dreams — an ice pick flying through the air and landing on its mark. Since the dream occurred when he was most excited and optimistic about his work, he saw the targets as symbols of optimism. His conclusion to the letter was most telling: "… a great many things in the painting are mysterious to me and inexplicable."

A companion work, *Cyclops* (fig. 7), includes another torso figure. Here, the deformed legs are separated by an irregular shape that may again suggest a sexual organ. A series of concentric circles appear

in the center of the head shape, giving the work its title. Baziotes recalled that this painting was inspired by a rhinoceros at the Bronx Zoo. Garnering important recognition for the artist, *Cyclops* was awarded the 1947 Walter M. Campana Memorial Purchase Prize at the Chicago Art Institute's 38th Annual Exhibition.

In *Night Form* (fig. 8), the dominant image is another macabre figure. Its torso also has deformed legs and arms. Unlike the images in the other two works, this figure has movement, for it appears to alight from the block form at the lower left. An ovoid shape within the head area again contains a series of concentric circles. *Night Form* is distinguished by the rhythm of its aggressively painted blue-black background and the simplified abstract shapes within the figure.

There are other works of the period that relate to the artist's revelations in his letter about *Dwarf.* The concentric circle-target shapes appear in *Pierrot*, 1947 (cat. no. 21), only this time in the head area, as in *Night Form*. It is a more playful work, in the whimsical spirit of Klee and Miró. The simplification of the body into a series of attenuated shapes, also seen in *Moon Animal*, 1950 (cat. no. 26), implies movement in the central figure.

Night Mirror, 1947 (cat. no. 23), combines many of these elements. The dominant figure of *Night Form* appears in the center; here the eye-psyche is represented by the sun-image that also appears in *Figures in Seascape*, 1947 (cat. no. 22). The vestiges of a linear automatism are evident in the pulsating form to the left. The figure on the right, floating in the scene like a protozoa, has anatomical forms within its contours that allude to female sexuality. The background is a worked surface much like that of *Night Form*.

The target shapes also appear in *Water Form*, 1947 (cat. no. 24), a more loosely painted work that has the quality of a dynamic watercolor abstraction. Here, jagged teeth stretch across the composition, not associated with any single form as in *Dwarf. Figures in Seascape*, 1947, is a compendium of Baziotes' artistic vocabulary to date — shapes with linear striations, a sun image, concentric circles, jagged teeth and curvilinear biomorphs.

"Biomorphic" became a familiar term to describe this new visual vocabulary. Alfred H. Barr, Jr. first used it in distinguishing the two main traditions of abstract art. One, based on the art and theories of Paul Cézanne and Georges Seurat, led to Cubism. The second derived from the art and theories of Paul Gauguin, his circle and the Nabis. Barr described the latter tradition as "… intuitional and emotional rather than intellectual, biomorphic rather than geometric in forms, curvilinear rather than rectilinear, decorative rather than structural, and romantic rather than classical in exaltation of the mystical, the spontaneous and the irrational."[19]

In a 1965 article in *ArtForum*, Lawrence Al-

7
William Baziotes
Cyclops, 1947
Oil on canvas,
48 x 40 in
The Art Institute
of Chicago, Walter
Campana Memorial
Collection, 1947.468

8
William Baziotes
Night Form, 1947
Oil on canvas,
47 3/4 x 36 1/8 in
St. Louis,
Washington
University Gallery
of Art. Gift of the
Frederic Olsen
Foundation, 1954

loway proposed the "Biomorphic Forties" as a convenient term to describe the time when the New York avant-garde had embraced Surrealism, and, like Baziotes, had sought a new source of inspiration.[20] In the search for a new subject matter that was connected to the subconscious and unconscious, biomorphism found life on the canvases of several artists. Many of them acknowledged shared influences — Dalí, Miró, Masson, Kandinsky, even Art Nouveau. Many chose paths to universal meaning already proposed by Freud and Jung. Of exceptional note were Mark Rothko, Adolph Gottlieb and Jackson Pollock.

Rothko's approach to content — a personalized myth-making steeped in Jung's archetype — and his use of biomorphic form was rich in the portrayal of transformation. Abstracted images of birds, humans or menageries of anthropomorphic creatures would all, as we see in *Slow Swirl at the Edge of the Sea*, 1944 (fig. 9), come into being with explosive energy. Occasionally Rothko would offer a specific myth in the title, as he did with *Syrian Bull*, (1943). However, his intent was never to replicate the literal myth:

> "If our titles recall the known myths of antiquity, we have used them again because they are the eternal symbols upon which we must fall back to express basic psychological ideas. They are the symbols of man's primitive fears and motivations, no matter in which land or what time, changing only in detail but never in substance…."[21]

With similar intent, Adolph Gottlieb used a Cubist-inspired grid in which he compartmentalized biomorphic forms and images derived from such diverse sources as African masks and American Indian art. Always loosely drawn, these divisions create energy between their parts. Often, the titles of these *pictographs* — like *Augury*, 1945 (fig. 10) — are evocative of myths, omens and mystery. Gottlieb, like Baziotes, achieved a coexistence of the primitive and the modern, imagination and nature, the abstract and the real.

For Jackson Pollock, a friend of Baziotes in the 1940s, Jung's psychoanalytic theories were of great importance. The connections between symbols and psychic exploration as well as the relationship between nature, ego and reality were his passions. From this, combined with Thomas Hart Benton's invaluable lessons in color and dynamic compositional rhythm, Pollock created his own remarkable body of work. In subject matter, it dealt with "everything from Picasso and Surrealism to Minoan moon goddesses and voracious, primal women [...] more generally, his forms loosely derive from primitivistic masks and totems and such elemental aspects of existence as birth and death."[22] The aggressive painterliness in Pollock's mature work is already evident in his paintings of the early 1940s, as we see in *The She-Wolf*, 1943 (fig. 11). Even when forms are reduced and simplified, as they are in *Two*, 1943–45 (fig. 12), there is tension that characterizes the interaction between the forms, a quality familiar in the work of another artist, Arshile Gorky, who shared with Pollock his enthusiasm for both Picasso and Kandinsky.[23]

In addition to Baziotes, Matta, Rothko, Gottlieb and Pollock, the most significant practitioners of biomorphism and myth-making include James Brooks, Fritz Bultman, Hans Burkhardt, Peter Busa, Dorothy Dehner, Jimmy Ernst, Helen Frankenthaler, Gerome Kamrowski, Philip Guston, David Hare, Willem de Kooning, Hans Hofmann, Lee Krasner, Wifredo Lam, Morris Louis, Robert Motherwell, Barnett Newman, Gordon Onslow Ford, Wolfgang Paalen, Richard Pousette-Dart, Ad Reinhardt, Charles Seliger, David Smith, Theodoros Stamos, Clyfford Still, Bradley Walker Tomlin, Esteban Vicente and Emerson Woelffer.

As Baziotes moved into the 1950s, his work evolved. Some qualities — like linear automatism — appear so transformed as to seem unconnected to their original source. Others components continued to receive his studied focus, as he explored imaginary worlds guided by the poet within. In 1949, he wrote:

"... Let the poet dream his dreams.
Yet, the poet must look at the world; must enter into other men's lives; must look at the earth and the sky; must examine the dust in the street; must walk through the world and his mirror."[24]

10
Adolph Gottlieb
Augury, 1945
Oil on canvas,
40 x 30 in
New York, Solomon
R. Guggenheim
Museum

23

Soul of a Poet, Heart of a Fighter

It is often enticing, even compelling, to use poetry and literary allusions to explain the meaning of works of art. Baziotes, this unique artist-poet-fighter, would likely have said that we are too eager to make concrete that which is elusive.

Baziotes the poet was a man who spent the most important part of his life in the studio, filling the gaps in his days with reading, occasional socializing, and quiet time along with his beloved wife Ethel. He regularly went to New York's 42nd Street library where he studied Leonardo's notebooks, Edgar Allen Poe and Charles Baudelaire.

In Reading, where he returned in the summer to paint, his friend and fellow Greek, Byron Vazakas, introduced him to Baudelaire, as well as to the Symbolist poets Paul Verlaine, Arthur Rimbaud and Stéphane Mallarmé, and the French critic and poet Paul Valéry.[25] Baziotes also knew the work of another poet and Reading native son, Wallace Stevens. He read detective novels, including those of Raymond Chandler, whose distinctive crime-solving techniques the artist admired. In fact, with overcoat, fedora and the ever-present cigarette dangling from his lips, Baziotes adopted, on occasion, a tough, 1940s detective persona for himself.

Baudelaire held a special place in Baziotes' life and work. As a spiritual companion, Baudelaire's poetry described experiences beyond conscious, everyday life, using evocative imagery and symbolism to create new sensations and states of mind. Decadence, the occult and the macabre were important in Baudelaire's imagination. *The Intimate Papers* and *The Flowers of Evil* were among Baziotes' favorite works. Barbara Cavaliere in "William Baziotes: The Subtlety of Life for the Artist" recounts one of Baziotes' favorite insights about Baudelaire that perhaps explains his affinity to the poet.

"The old occult writers held that the evil thoughts of others beget phantoms in the air that can make themselves bodies out of our fear and haunt even our waking moments. These are the shapes of terror that haunted Baudelaire."[26]

Baziotes' spiritual journey was an exploration of opposites — the exquisite dichotomies in the human condition intrigued him. That sensibility was expressed in his reaction to the Picasso retrospective exhibition at the Museum of Modern Art in 1939:

"Well, I looked at Picasso until I could smell his armpits and the cigarette smoke on his breath. Finally, in front of one picture — a bone figure on a beach — I got it. I saw that the figure was not his real subject. The plasticity wasn't either — although the plasticity was great. No. Picasso had uncovered a feverishness in himself and is painting it — a feverishness of death and beauty."[27]

A decade later, in the October 1948 issue of *Tiger's Eye*, Baziotes' verse carried the same spirit:

"To be inspired. That is the thing.
To be possessed; to be bewitched.
To be obsessed. That is the thing.
To be inspired."[28]

Much of Baziotes' writing was about the artist translating inspiration to production. In "I Cannot Evolve Any Concrete Theory," he wrote:

"Today it's possible to paint one canvas with the calmness of an ancient Greek and the next with the anxiety of a Van Gogh. Either of these emotions, and any in between, is valid to me [...] I work on many canvases at once. In the morning I line them up against the wall of my studio. Some speak: some do not. They are my mirrors. They tell me what I am like at the moment."[29]

Both fear and courage were powerful attributes for Baziotes. Ethel Baziotes recalls that when her husband was most fearful, he would remark: "All men of imagination are afraid of madness." The artist showed his concern for the public's appreciation of his work in a statement he attributed to Baudelaire: "I have a horror of being easily understood." This deep respect for courage in overcoming fear is shown in the words from the memoirs of General William Tecumseh Sherman that were cut into the artist's tombstone: "I would define true courage to be a perfect sensibility of the full measure of danger and a mental willingness to endure it." This attitude also explains why Baziotes' highest admiration was reserved for Piet Mondrian, whose intense dedication to his work was similarly courageous.

In Baziotes the poet there is a symbiosis with Baziotes the fighter. We know that the artist learned the ways of the streets and met its full cast of characters. He boxed occasionally as a teenager

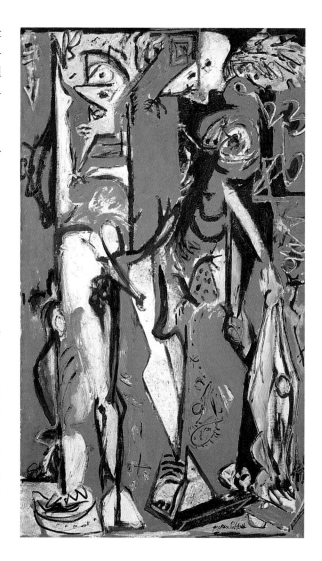

12
Jackson Pollock
Two, 1943–45
Oil on canvas,
75,9 x 43,3 in
Venice, Peggy
Guggenheim
Collection

25

at the local YMCA and almost every night when he worked for the *Reading Times*. In later years, he read boxing magazines and followed the sport.[30]

He found inspiration in the boxer's struggle. The William and Ethel Baziotes Papers at the Archives of American Art contain a hand-written note by the artist recording a statement by the earlier heavyweight champion, Gene Tunney.

"If there's any extreme form of individualism, it's ring fighting. You wage your own battle all by yourself. No partners, no comrades in there with you. Like dying, you fight alone. So consider the prizefighter as a spiritualist individualist, a solitary soul in travail."[31]

Baziotes' commitment to nature and primordial forces found a metaphor in the boxing arena. Sigfried Giedion, the pioneer modern theorist active in the 1930s and 1940s, offered a parallel for Baziotes' "solitary soul in travail," one with which the Surrealists and Dadaists could concur:

"Whereas in primitive eras magic, myth and religious power provided man with a spiritual armor against a hostile environment, today he stands stripped and naked."[32]

Baudelaire offered another perspective of spiritual isolation in his poem, "The Albatross:"

"The poet is like the prince of the clouds
Who haunts the tempest and laughs at the archer
Exiled on the ground in the midst of jeers,
His giant wings prevent him from walking."[33]

Writing for a 1954 symposium on the creative process, Baziotes said that the artist is never isolated from dialogue with his own work: "I work on eight or 10 paintings at once; at the same time, I draw and make pastels and watercolors." He also wrote of his appreciation of the value of collaboration: "There is always an unconscious collaboration among artists [...] the artist who imagines himself a Robinson Crusoe is either a primitive or a fool." Later in the symposium he put his personal association with artists at a distance: "The good artists of my gener-

ation are, by this time, in kingdoms of their own making."[34]

Metamorphosis

The early 1950s was a time of transition in Baziotes' life. He had long since left Art of This Century and become associated with Samuel Kootz, whose gallery was also supportive of his work.[35] True friendships would be elusive in this period, for many of his friends and fellow-artists were on different paths. Some, like Matta and Masson, returned to Europe. For others, death came too early — Arshile Gorky in 1947, Bradley Walker Tomlin in 1953 and Jackson Pollock in 1956. Rothko, Gottlieb, Pollock and Motherwell ventured far from Baziotes aesthetically, choosing gesture and surface manipulation to create expressive form, while Baziotes continued to employ concrete images as a point of departure.

Baziotes spoke of his growing isolation in veiled terms in 1952:

"I think the reason we begin in a different way is that this particular time has gotten to a point where the artist feels like a gambler. He does something on the canvas and takes a chance in the hope that something important will be revealed."[36]

The gamble that Baziotes took was the evolution of his work away from gestural abstraction and toward a re-imagining of nature that can best be described as metamorphosis. In this sense, the term meant more than simply change. It was, rather, the emerging of something new and different. His pictures became arenas of transformed life.

In the real world Baziotes saw crocodiles, rhinoceroses, shellfish, spiders and amoeba; he also saw dioramas, specimens and illustrations of a myriad of prehistoric land and sea creatures. In his imagination, he understood the essential energy of nature in its primordial form. Now, in his mature work, he would give us dioramas of the imagination, an empirical view of new worlds.

The settings for his paintings are often aquatic, giving us the sense of looking into an antique aquarium. In mysterious oceans, creatures akin to microscopic life float by in quiet rhythms, as in *Sea*

Forms, 1951 (cat. no. 28), and and *Sleep*, 1952 (cat. no. 31). Harmonies of musical color dominate many works, like the emerald-green waters of *Moby Dick*, 1955 (cat. no. 39), and the cool currents of *Aquatic*, 1961 (cat. no. 56).

Referring to this marine sensibility, Ethel Baziotes recalls one of her husband's favorite sayings: "My work is like the Caribbean Sea — beautiful, serene, and exotic on the surface. And all the time below are the sharks."[37]

There are terrestrial settings as well, sometimes with familiar landscape elements, like the sun image in *Moon Animal*, 1950 (cat. no. 26), and the vertical cliff in *Flame*, 1954 (cat. no. 37). The firmly rooted tree image in *The Flesh Eaters*, 1952 (cat. no. 30), creates tension between the two biomorphic forms. In *Red Landscape*, 1956 (cat. no. 41), a spider-form crawls up through the earth-toned ground; the three-pronged form on the left has already penetrated the misty green sky, threatening the cloud-shaped creature.

With foresight and a Surrealist's sensibility, Baziotes spoke eloquently in 1947 about the metamorphosis of forms in his pictures:

"Each painting has its own way of evolving. One may start with a few color areas on the canvas; another with a myriad of lines, another with a profusion of colors […] Once I sense the suggestion I begin to paint intuitively. The suggestion then becomes a phantom that must be caught and made real. As I work, or when the painting is finished, the subject reveals itself."[38]

His biomorphic forms are now remarkably diverse. Certain large images recall fish and prehistoric creatures, appearing in various states: transparent, as in *Sleep*; semi-transparent in *Grotto*, 1952 (cat. no. 32); or opaque in *Moby Dick*. Other images are purely linear, like the insect form in *Red Landscape*; the jellyfish tendrils in *Phantom*, 1953 (cat. no. 34); or the starburst-web in *The Pond*, 1955 (cat. no. 40). Complex forms, like the tentacled creature in *The Flesh Eaters*, the multiwinged bird in *Primeval Landscape*, 1953 (cat. no. 35), or the wave-shaped sea form in *The Beach* (fig. 13), are reminiscent of specimens on view at the Museum of Natural History.[39]

Baziotes' small collection of folk art was also an inspiration in the development of forms. His attraction to an early American carved snake appears as a serpentine form in many paintings, including *Spider*, 1956 (cat. no. 42), and *Dusk*, 1958 (cat. no. 49). In "Four Sources of Inspiration," Mona Hadler noted that a sculpture in his collection of a noble and powerful draft horse called a Percheron was a possible inspiration for the large image in *Dusk*.[40] But Hadler noted further that one of the artist's favorite sculptures at the Metropolitan, an eighteenth-century B.C. Greek geometric-period horse, was a more likely source; the artist would have responded to its appealing combination of primitivism and eloquence.

Baziotes brought his metaphorical world to life through a remarkable depiction of light and an extraordinarily sophisticated use of color. His decision to eliminate brushstrokes on his canvases by a careful, repetitive rubbing of the oil surface allowed subtle highlights to emerge; the resulting light and dark passages created undefined depth in the composition.

Light has the strength of a life-force in several works. The moon's light overcomes the sun and bathes the figure in *Moon Animal*. The blue ovoid to the left in *Desert Landscape*, 1951 (cat. no. 27), glows like a powerful beacon that touches the figures on the right. The light flowing from the tonal shape set on the horizon in *Primeval Landscape* effects a metamorphosis, transforming the cocoon creature into the winged bird. The absence of light has the opposite effect, as we see in the dark, ovoid death symbol in *Pompeii*, 1955 (fig. 14).

Baziotes used darkness as an element to enhance the character of mystery in his work. In *Underground*, 1951 (cat. no. 29), the dark background intensifies the radiant illumination of the image. Within the dark depths of *Grotto*, brilliant yellow light reaches up and seems to threaten several swirling images. The dark background in *Phantom*, brings the three images to the foreground, forcing them into a compressed space; the result is a heightened sense of interaction, with the spidery form particularly threatening as it hovers above the other forms. In *Green Night*, 1957 (cat. no. 45), the black in the background is countered by the richness and vibrancy of the greens. Late in his life, in 1959, Baziotes explained his obsession with mystery:

13
William Baziotes
The Beach, 1955
Oil on canvas,
36 x 48 in
New York,
Collection of the
Whitney Museum
of American Art

"It is the mysterious that I love in painting. It is the stillness and the silence. I want my pictures to take effect very slowly, to obsess and to haunt."[41]

Baziotes found this same haunting quality in *Adam* (circa 1490–95) by the Italian Tullio Lombardo, which he visited often at the Metropolitan. He was entranced by the dramatic contrast between the hand that holds the apple with sublime delicacy, and the face, with its look of broken innocence.

Not surprisingly, in his desire to let pictures "take effect very slowly," Baziotes rarely specified the meaning of his later work. One exception is *Pompeii*, 1955. The artist explained the source of his inspiration for the work, recently purchased by the Museum of

Modern Art, in a letter to Alfred H. Barr, Jr. of 6 November 1955.[42] He noted that since 1953 he had been interested in Roman civilization, especially its "decadence, subtlety and languor" and in Roman wall paintings with their "veiled melancholy." He felt that the background of the upper part of the picture was related to geology, since so much of Roman art was made of stone, marble and minerals. He later noted: "The large gray spiked form rising from the bottom of the picture is to me the symbol of death and ruin. And finally the black ovoid form is the symbol of fire, lava and destruction." The source of the Pompeian-red color in his painting likely derives from the Metropolitan's collection of antique paintings from two villas at Boscoreale on the slopes of Mount Vesuvius.

Though Baziotes never made direct reference to his painting *Moby Dick*, he did refer to it obliquely in an article in the *Reading Record*:

"You wouldn't understand a novel like 'Moby Dick' at one glance. It's the same with painting. It must be studied over a long period of time. The more you look at it, the more it unfolds."[43]

Since Baziotes considered titles to be merely associative and assigned them after completion of the painting, there is no reason to apply a literal interpretation to the few paintings with specific titles. In a series of interviews with Donald Paneth in 1952, Baziotes made comments on the content of several paintings:

"'Pierrot' [...] expresses an adolescent figure, naïve and innocent, walking through a gloomy landscape. 'The Somnambulist' is a picture of the strange Proustian state between sleep and wakefulness, a white figure in the foreground is all sharpness — the reality you feel — while the background is violet and dreamy and lyrical. 'The Falcon' is some kind of bird on a cliff, a condor or vulture, looking down upon the world with a mean little eye, a picture of certain evil things in the world with the smell of death about them. 'Night Forms' is a picture with an eye and a lot of spiky looking things; it's very primeval, as if the teeth and skulls of some ancient people had been found in a cave. 'Green Form' is a nude bending over a waterfall. Kind of pagan picture with a feeling of the primeval and ancestors. Silence, emptiness all around."[44]

Interspersed among the later canvases are some extraordinary examples of drawing and watercolor. Baziotes enjoyed the two mediums, for he was at once freed from the intimidation of scale and the constraints of wet paint. He often quoted Jean-Auguste-Dominique Ingres' famous dictum, "Drawing is the probity of art" along with his own "Drawing is a labyrinthian journey."

In the 1930s, Baziotes discussed several ideas about drawings in his 94-page sketchbook, probably related to his classes at the National Academy

of Design. A few excerpts remind us of the rigors of the studio and illustrate the emphasis on craftsmanship over a free form, Surrealistic approach.

"Look long at what you are going to draw, and thoroughly understand at least two things about it — the proportion of the component parts, both internally to themselves and relatively to the whole subject; and then the main directions of its different parts to and from you as well as sideways [...]
Make up your mind fully about what you are going to do with a line before beginning to draw it; then draw it with unhesitating determination. Do all the hesitating before you begin. Think a line out before executing it; choose just what kind of details of nature it shall represent; its length, direction, and kind of curvature [...]
Weakness in drawing is largely lack of decided and completed intentions before commencing [...]
Remember that a painting is but a rhythmic arrangement of forms and color, so our every effort must be toward a maintenance of the unity of rhythm."[45]

Though the drawings *Untitled (Study for Moby Dick)*, 1953–54 (cat. no. 36), and *Cobra*, 1957 (cat. no. 43), have literal references in the titles, they are not blueprints for paintings. His watercolors and drawings are more like sketches, quick studies of relationships that were created in the studio as part of his routine exercises. For example, in *Flesh Form and Web*, 1959 (cat. no. 51), a very loosely painted work with broad strokes of fluid watercolor, even the tack marks remain. Its two central forms vie for dominance, as two serpentine lines stretch across the surface. The two watercolors from 1958 (cat. nos. 47-48) are more controlled and tightly painted than *Flesh Form and Web*. There are more images, as well, as though the artist is working out ideas and relationships for dense and complicated compositions. A few drawings, like *Prehistoric*, 1957 (cat. no. 46), emphasize the juxtaposition of light and dark passages — in this case to the unusual point that within the contours of the large, central figure, the untouched watercolor paper shows through. The last of the watercolors, from 1961 and 1962 (cat. no. 57), are studies in tone and hue whose simplification of forms heads toward pure abstraction.

Baziotes the colorist and Baziotes the image-maker were superbly at work in the late, monumental paintings. In *Autumn Leaf*, 1959 (cat. no. 53), he established tension by placing the insect form in the foreground along the left vertical edge of the canvas, while the leaf-shaped life form rests in the middle ground to the right. Emerging from the cocoon-like image below it, the black insect seems ready to spring, and to seek sustenance from the white-toned life form. The distribution of forms here is similar to the composition of *The Flesh Eaters*. The significant difference lies in the coloration; Baziotes has moved away from the earlier painting's garish coloration to a more sophisticated treatment luminous fall hues and a fragile brilliance of golden tones.

In *Mariner*, 1960–61 (cat. no. 55), Baziotes gave renewed life to a protean environment through a clever manipulation of the figure-ground relationship. A horizon line is reinforced by creating a reflection of the figure on the right. But it is an imperfect reflection, with only a slight resemblance to the original, as though it too has transformed. On the left, an image recalling the foreground figure of the earlier *Pompeii* is placed below the horizon, with no reflection, and within the watery lower ground.

Aquatic is pure poetry. Specific geological and topographical elements are removed. The picture plane has a uniform tonality. Its images float without conflict; it is quietude and peace of the most romantic sort, and another indication of his further move toward abstraction.

With *Scepter*, 1960–61 (cat. no. 54), Baziotes reached a milestone, endowing his images with symbolic intent. The elegant, white form to the left is the scepter of the title, an emblem of authority and power. It dominates the canvas through its placement in the foreground of a lightly toned field. Lurking in the shadows to the right and below the center line is a darker mass, which, by virtue of contrast, becomes the opposing force. It is animated by a subtle heightening of color on the left side of the contour and a darkening on the right. A floating linear element in the upper right secures asymmetrical balance.

Baziotes relied here on psychological mainstays — light and dark, elegance and crudeness — in setting his two main forms against each other. The scepter emerges from the light with dominating size and presence, while the dark mass lurks in the background. In *Scepter*, the simplicity of the composition and the refinement of the forms bring us to the essential conflict of good and evil. These are no longer primordial images but everlasting symbols.

Like so many heroes and heroines of Abstract Expressionism, Baziotes was a dedicated, passionate painter for whom little else was of the same importance. For him, the act of painting required a special reverence and patience, a meditative state that allowed the imagination and the unconscious to find expression. His best work recalls the past, present and future in its synthesis of primitive art, modern art, the old masters and antiquity. In the months before his death in New York on 6 June 1963, that passion ebbed; there are few paintings, for his loss of strength had seriously curtailed his ability to paint.

Baziotes left us, his viewers, with a special obligation. We must give his works time for contemplation, what Ethel Baziotes calls the "art of lingering." His metaphors for birth, life and death are gently phrased in painterly story-telling. In Baudelaire, we find the kindred spirit.[46] From "Invitation to the Voyage" (*The Flowers of Evil*):

"There, there is nothing else but grace and measure,
Richness, quietness and pleasure."

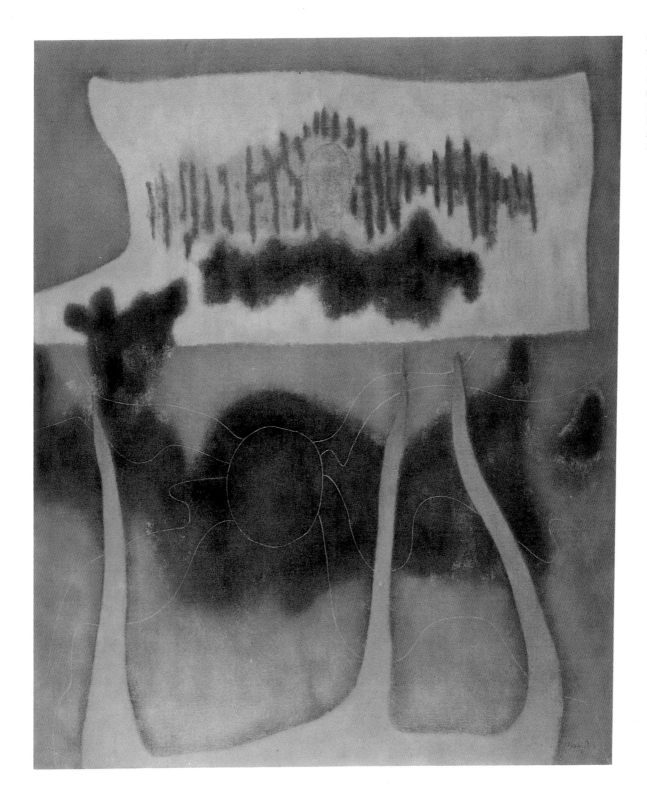

14
William Baziotes
Pompeii, 1955
Oil on canvas,
60 x 48 in
New York, The
Museum of Modern
Art, Mrs. Bertram
Smith Fund, 1955

[1] W.B. Scott, P.M. Rutkoff, *New York Modern, The Arts and the City*, Baltimore, Johns Hopkins University Press, 1999, pp. 171, 181.

[2] Information about Baziotes' youth comes from discussions with the artist's widow Ethel Baziotes, during the years 1977 to 2004; and from Donald Paneth's unpublished manuscript based on interviews with the artist from February to July 1952. See William and Ethel Baziotes Papers, 1916-1992, Archives of American Art, Smithsonian Institution, Washington, D.C., microfilm N 70-21. The Paneth manuscript includes the comment that the article was turned down for publication by *New World Writing* in 1962 because Baziotes would not give written authorization.

[3] D. Paneth, *op. cit.*, p. 9.

[4] *Ibidem.*

[5] W. Baziotes in "Symposium: The Creative Process," *Art Digest*, vol. 28, no. 8, 15 January 1954, pp. 16, 33. Participants, as listed in the publication, included William Baziotes, Stuart Davis, Jose de Creeft, Rollin Crampton, Yves Tanguy, Peter Blume, George Grosz and Larry Rivers, a former student of Baziotes.

[6] Earlier Surrealist shows included the one-person exhibitions of the work of Giorgio de Chirico and Joan Miró at Valentine Gallery in 1927. In 1930, the same year that Breton published the second Surrealist manifesto, the Museum of Modern Art opened a large exhibition devoted to Paul Klee; his interest in fantasy and the imagination associated him with the Surrealists. The first major Surrealist-group exhibition in America was held in Hartford, Connecticut, in 1931; Dalí, de Chirico, Ernst, Miró, Picasso, Survage and Masson were represented.

[7] Interestingly, in 1936, Julien Levy championed Joseph Cornell as "one of the very few Americans at the present time who fully and creatively understands the surrealist viewpoint." See J. Levy, *Surrealism*, New York, Black Sun Press, 1936, p. 28.

[8] Irving Sandler in *The Triumph of American Painting* argued that a single act of World War II, the fall of Paris to the Germans in 1940, made New York the international capital of art. See I. Sandler, *The Triumph of American Painting*, New York, Harper & Row, 1976, p. 31.

[9] *Dutch Interior II* is of special importance because Peggy Guggenheim purchased the painting in 1940, and it was regularly on view at Art of This Century gallery. Masson's *Meditation on an Oak Leaf*, 1942, was likely familiar to Baziotes due to his friendship with the artist. The painting became more widely known when the Museum of Modern Art acquired it in 1950.

[10] A. Breton, *Manifeste du Surréalisme*, Paris, Editions KRA, 1929, p. 46. In his later book *What Is Surrealism* (London, Faber and Faber Ltd., 1936; translated by D. Gascoyne; p. 51), Breton makes the point that this definition, which also appeared in his 1924 manifesto, should be amended to read "... free from *conscious* moral or aesthetic preoccupations."

[11] The influence of automatism in the formation of Abstract Expressionism is well covered in Martica Sawin's essay, "The Cycloptic Eye, Pataphysics and the Possible: Transformations of Surrealism," in P. Schimmel *et al.*, *The Interpretive Link: Abstract Surrealism into Abstract Expressionism, Works on Paper, 1938-1948*, Newport Beach, California, Newport Harbor Art Museum, 1986, pp. 37–42.

[12] In an interview conducted by Sidney Simon in Minneapolis in 1966, Peter Busa gave credit to Baziotes for dripping paint on canvas even before Pollock. In the same interview, Matta noted that he saw work by Max Ernst in 1942 in which he was dripping paint from cans with holes in the bottom onto canvas laid out on the floor. From "Concerning the Beginnings of the New York School: 1939-1943 – An Interview with Peter Busa and Matta, Conducted by Sidney Simon in Minneapolis in December 1966," *Art International*, vol. XI/6, summer 1967, pp. 17–18.

[13] Baziotes was familiar with the 1939 edition of *The Notebooks of Leonardo da Vinci*. See R. Carlton Hobbs, G. Levin, *Abstract Expressionism: The Formative Years*, Ithaca, New York, Cornell University Press, 1981, p. 61.

[14] For a description of his technique, see J. Arp, *On My Way – Poetry and Essays, 1912-1947*, New York, Wittenborn, Schultz, 1948, pp. 51, 77. This volume contains an eloquent and insightful introduction by Robert Motherwell.

[15] William and Ethel Baziotes Papers... cit., microfilm N 70-21.

[16] H. Janis, R. Blesh, *Collage: Personalities, Concepts Techniques*, Philadelphia, Chilton Co., 1962, p. 171

[17] S. Terenzio (ed.), *The Collected Writings of Robert Motherwell*, Berkeley and Los Angeles, California, University of Los Angeles Press, 1999, p. 3.

[18] William and Ethel Baziotes Papers... cit., microfilm N 70-21.

[19] A.H. Barr, Jr., *Cubism and Abstract Art*, New York, Museum of Modern Art, 1936, p. 19.

[20] First appearing in "The Biomorphic Forties," *ArtForum*, vol. IV, September 1965, and expanded in P. Schimmel *et al.*, *op. cit.*, pp. 33–36.

[21] Mark Rothko, in a 1943 letter to *The New York Times*, co-authored with Adolph Gottlieb and Barnett Newman. See *Myths and Symbols* [online], Washington, D.C., National Gallery of Art. [Cited 15 January 2004]. Available from World Wide Web (http: www.nag.gov/feature/rothko/).

[22] S. Hunter, "An American Master: Jackson Pollock, 1930-1949, Myth and Reality," in *Pollock's America, Jackson Pollock in Venice, The Irascibles and the New York School*, Milan, Skira Editore, 2002, pp. 59–60.

[23] Though Arshile Gorky is often portrayed in art historical literature as the link between Surrealism and Abstract Expressionism, as well as a key proponent of automatism, there is no documentation for significant interaction between Gorky and Baziotes. In her new book on Gorky, author Hayden Herrera notes that Gorky was present at the 1942 gala inauguration of the Art of This Century gallery at 30 West 57th Street, which Baziotes likely attended. Gorky and Baziotes both exhibited at Howard Putzel's 67 Gallery in May 1945 in "A Problem for Critics," which included the work of the older generation of avant-garde painters — Masson, Matta, Miró, Arp, Picasso and Tamayo — and the new generation of Americans — Pollock, Rothko, Motherwell, Krasner, Gottlieb, Hofmann, Pousette-Dart and Charles Seliger. See H. Herrera, *Arshile Gorky, His Life and Work*, New York, Farrar, Straus and Giroux, 2003, pp. 288, 482.

[24] W. Baziotes, "The Artist and His Mirror," *Right Angle*, vol. III, no. 2, Washington, D.C., June 1949, p. 3.

[25] M. Hadler, "William Baziotes, Four Sources of Inspiration," in *William Baziotes Retrospective Exhibition*, Newport Harbor, California, Newport Harbor, 1978, pp. 82, 84. Hadler cites other influential literature: Proust's *Remembrance of Things Past*; the work of Arthur Schnitzler; and G.N.M. Tyrrell's *The Personality of Man*, which is referenced in the artist's teaching notes from Hunter College. In a 1 March 2004 conversation with the author, artist Charles Seliger recalled that he and Baziotes were reading Wassermann's *The World's Illusion* in the 1940s. Seliger described this work as "dense with intricate relationships, ennui, self analysis, makes Thomas Mann seem simple."

[26] B. Cavaliere, "William Baziotes: The Subtlety of Life for the Artist," in *William Baziotes Retrospective Exhibition*, Newport Harbor, California, Newport Harbor Art Museum, pp. 36, 60, 29fn. Quotation from T.R. Smith's introduction to *Baudelaire: His Prose and Poetry*, New York, Random House, 1919, p. 35. This edition was in Baziotes' home library.

[27] R. Blesh, *Modern Art U.S.A.*, New York, Alfred A. Knopf, 1956, pp. 268–69. Blesh bought Baziotes' *The Mirror at Midnight I*, 1942 circa, from Art of This Century in 1945.

[28] W. Baziotes in *Tiger's Eye*, vol. I, no. 5, Westport, Connecticut, October 1948, p. 35.

[29] W. Baziotes in "I Cannot Evolve Any Concrete Theory," *Possibilities*, vol. I, no. 1, New York, Wittenborn, Schultz Inc., winter 1947–48, p. 2.

[30] Donald Paneth's manuscript includes a comment by Baziotes on his fellow pugilists: "A great many good painters used to box. Miró, Derain, Braque, Vlaminck." See D. Paneth, *op. cit.*, p. 19. William and Ethel Baziotes Papers... cit., microfilm N 70-21.

[31] *Ibidem*, microfilm N 70-21.

[32] S.S. Giedion, "The Symbol in Primeval Art," *The Eternal Present: The Beginnings of Art*, vol. I, Washington, D.C., National Gallery of Art, 1962, p. 80. Giedion (1888-1968) was an art and architectural historian and outspoken modernist. His influential lectures of the late 1930s were reprinted in *Time, Space and Architecture: The Growth of a New Tradition* in 1947. *The Eternal Present* includes the A.W. Mellon Lectures, presented at the National Gallery of Art in 1957.

[33] C. Baudelaire, "The Albatross," *The Flowers of Evil*, Norfolk, Connecticut, New Directions, 1955, p. 10. *Albatross* is also the title of a painting by Baziotes; other paintings with Baudelaire poem titles include *Vampire*, *Balcony* and *Phantom*.

[34] W. Baziotes in "Symposium: the Creative Process" cit., pp. 16, 34.

[35] Samuel Kootz Gallery handled Baziotes' work until 1958; after a brief period with Saidenberg Gallery, Marlborough Gallery became his dealer and initially represented the estate. Thereafter, the estate was represented by Blum-Helman Gallery. Currently Joseph Helman Gallery, New York City, represents the estate.

[36] R. Motherwell, A. Reinhardt (eds.), *Modern Artists in America*, New York, Wittenborn, Schultz Inc., 1952, pp. 11, 13–17.

[37] The original reference comes from the 1949 Museum of Modern Art correspondence. Baziotes credits this comment to a critique (source unknown) of the work of Ludwig von Beethoven.

[38] W. Baziotes in "I Cannot Evolve Any Concrete Theory" cit., p. 2.

[39] In a recent conversation, Charles Seliger recalled one of his conversations with Baziotes

in the 1940s: both were reading Jean Henri Fabre's *The Life of the Spider*. Seliger noted that the book's true value was in its remarkable ability to treat insect life in poetic, human terms.

[40] M. Hadler, *op. cit.*, p. 96.

[41] W. Baziotes, "Notes on Painting," *It Is*, no. 4, autumn 1959, p. 11.

[42] The letter accompanied an information form from the Museum of Modern Art's Department of Painting and Sculpture. Reprinted from Museum of Modern Art Archives in William and Ethel Baziotes Papers… cit., microfilm N 70-21. Lee Nordness in a short essay on the artist in *Art USA Now* said that the spidery line symbolized the volcano and that the three spiked forms were "… the three petrified legs of the famous Pompeian canine, faithful to his master, raised in death." See L. Nordness, A.S. Weller, *Art USA Now*, vol. II, New York, Viking Press, 1963, p. 261.

[43] Reprinted from the Whitney Museum Paper, from an article by Bob Gregg (1959), in William and Ethel Baziotes Papers… cit., microfilm N 646. Interestingly, Jackson Pollock, who was fond of the novel *Moby Dick*, created two works in the 1940s with that title. One, a painting now called *Pasiphae*, 1943, was originally titled *Moby Dick*; it was rechristened by James Johnson Sweeney, who got Pollock to change the title after recounting the legend of Minos of Crete. The second is a gouache from 1945 titled *Blue (Moby Dick)*. See B. Robertson, *Jackson Pollock*, New York, Abrams, 1960, pp. 138, 148.

[44] D. Paneth, *op. cit.*, pp. 8–9.

[45] From *Sketchbook 1*, 1998.132.1-94 in the collection of the National Gallery of Art, Washington, D.C. Though undated, these sketchbooks are likely the product of classes, if not a class assignment, with Leon Kroll at the National Academy of Design from 1933–36.

[46] C. Baudelaire, *op. cit.*, pp. 68–69.

Natural Painter and All Painter — The Emergence of William Baziotes

Jasper Sharp

William Baziotes,
circa 1940

One of the earliest letters written on the newly printed stationery of Art of This Century, Peggy Guggenheim's celebrated New York museum-gallery, was addressed to William Baziotes. Dated 14 April 1942 — more than six months before the gallery opened — it was sent by his good friend Jimmy Ernst from the East 51st Street townhouse in which Peggy and Jimmy's father Max had settled late the previous year. The younger Ernst was at the time working as an assistant to Peggy, handling correspondence, keeping her books, fielding press enquiries and assisting with the production of the first catalogue of her collection.

"Dear Bill, Breton just asked me to ask you for a drawing, gouache or the likes. There is going to be a show of drawings etc. by all the collaborators in the Surrealist group at the Weyhe Gallery. Now don't you dare and play the inferior or unimportant, if you refuse to make a drawing I shall never try to guess any swing-band on your radio again. Can you call me tomorrow around noon? Yours, Jimmy."[1]

The exhibition did not, in the end, take place, but the nature of the letter's invitation was hugely significant. For Baziotes, a dedicated and determined painter not yet thirty years old, it represented the first acknowledgment of his work by the influential leader of the community of European Surrealist émigrés.

Within a few months a second, more momentous opportunity presented itself. At Peggy's suggestion, André Breton was approached by the French couturier Elsa Schiaparelli to organize a fundraising Surrealist exhibition in New York in aid of the Coordinating Council of French Relief Societies. On 7 September 1942, Breton wrote to Baziotes inviting him to propose a work for inclusion in the exhibition, to be named "First Papers of Surrealism." The same letter included a checklist of artists whose work was to be presented. Tucked in between the names of renowned Europeans such as Jean Arp, Victor Brauner, Giorgio de Chirico, Paul Delvaux, Alberto Giacometti, Paul Klee, René Magritte, André Masson, Joan Miró, Pablo Picasso, and Yves Tanguy, were those of a handful of emerging Americans including Baziotes, John Goodwin, David Hare, Gerome Kamrowski, Robert Motherwell, Ralph Nelson, Barbara Reis, and Kay Sage.[2] Baziotes accepted at once, offering Breton a recent work, *Leonardo da Vinci's Butterfly* (1942; cat. no. 6), which took its place in the theatrical installation designed by Marcel Duchamp (fig. 1).[3]

Less than two weeks later, seven floors above a grocer's shop on West 57th Street, Baziotes and his young wife Ethel attended the gala opening of Art of This Century. Designed by the Austrian architect Frederick Kiesler, principally to display Peggy's collection of predominantly European modern art, the gallery was also intended to be "a center where artists will be welcome and where they can feel that they are cooperating in establishing a research center for new ideas" (fig. 2).[4]

"The drama of the scene was overpowering," Ethel later recalled. "The presence of Europe at that

1

Exhibition
catalogue, "First
Papers of
Surrealism," 1942,
designed by Marcel
Duchamp

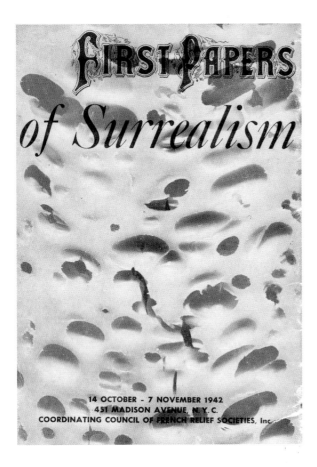

point [...] the momentum was making everybody spin a little."[5] The two were frequent guests at Peggy's soirées, first at her Beekman Place townhouse, and then at the duplex apartment she shared with Kenneth Macpherson at 155 East 61st Street.[6]

Exhilarated but by no means overwhelmed by what they saw, a small group of these younger artists interpreted Peggy's call as a direct invitation to exhibit their work in her gallery. At the heart of the group was Roberto Matta, a Chilean painter who had arrived in New York in October 1939. Matta and Baziotes met in May of the following year at the 10th Street loft of photographer and filmmaker Francis Lee, a popular hangout for American artists and the Surrealist émigrés who had been arriving in the city since the late 1930s. Some time later Matta introduced Baziotes to Motherwell, recently returned from Mexico. The three artists began to meet regularly, moving to Matta's apartment on 12th Street following Lee's draft. They were joined by others including Peter Busa, Kamrowski and Jackson Pollock, and together experimented with automatist techniques (fig. 3).[7] Matta was very much the catalyst, guiding their efforts and sharing with them his experience of similar endeavors in the company of Breton, Esteban Francés, Gordon Onslow Ford and Yves Tanguy during the spring and summer of 1939 at the Château Chemilliere in Brittany. Often in attendance at the group's meetings, usually held on Saturday nights, were several of the artist's wives. Motherwell recalled at least one evening in the spring of 1942 during which he and his wife Maria, William and Ethel Baziotes, and Lee Krasner and Jackson Pollock together created a series of automatic poems.[8]

The confidence derived from such practises was galvanized by what they perceived to be a divergence on the part of the European Surrealists from the original, literary principles of Breton's 1924 manifesto. Baziotes, Matta and Motherwell went as far as to propose the idea of a group exhibition at Art of This Century based on the principles of "abstract automatism" and intended to "show up the then middle-aged Surrealists."[9] Busa, Kamrowski, Willem de Kooning, and Pollock were invited to join, and Peggy was sounded out. She was understandably hesitant, given the assertive presence at the time of many of said "middle-aged Surrealists" in both her gallery and personal life. Breton, Marcel Duchamp and Max Ernst were among the more prominent voices to whom she was then listening, while her brief marriage to the latter placed her at the very heart of the Surrealist émigré *milieu*.

Her subsequent estrangement from Ernst, however, and the appointment of Howard Putzel as the new secretary of Art of This Century, established a climate in which Peggy's stated aim of "serving the future instead of recording the past" could at last be achieved.[10] At Putzel's suggestion, Peggy extended an invitation to a small group of American artists to produce work for an "Exhibition of Collage" to be held at the gallery. The idea of the show came from a similar enterprise mounted some five years previously at her London gallery Guggenheim Jeune, where, with the help of her friend, the artist and collector Roland Penrose, Peggy had organized an exhibition of collages and papiers collés in November 1938.[11] On that occasion, a nucleus of established European artists, such as Arp, Georges Braque, Max Ernst, Juan Gris, Picasso and Kurt Schwitters, who had pioneered the medium's development, were joined by a group of younger, relatively unknown British artists. The exhibition's success, and the fact that her own collection permanently displayed at Art of This Century now contained remarkable examples of works by those same Europeans, convinced her to repeat the experiment in New York. Despite more than thirty years of practice in Europe, collage was a technique little seen in the United States, obliging critics to provide basic introductions to this "unusual French method of cutting out various pictures and pasting them to ornamental plates, trays and boxes."[12] The exhibition presented the work of thirty-seven artists, and was the first devoted to the collage medium ever to have been organized in the United States.[13]

Alongside the more historical works by European artists, priced as high as $2500, hung a selection of fresh, first-time collages and papiers collés for sale at as little as $25, by the younger American artists.[14] They included Baziotes, Hare (at the time a photographer), Motherwell, Pollock, and Ad Reinhardt. Motherwell, whose name was omitted from the exhibition's original announcement card, recalled that Peggy had invited himself, Baziotes and Pollock to

2
Peggy Guggenheim seated on a Correalist rocker, Art of This Century, photographed by Berenice Abbott, New York, 1942

submit works in February 1943. "She asked me if any of the three of us had made collages, and when I said no, in a spirit of the greatest spontaneous generosity and benigness she said, why don't the three of you try collage, and if you like what you do, I will show it. Which we did and she did."[15]

While Motherwell and Pollock chose to experiment together in the latter's Greenwich Village studio, Baziotes worked alone to produce *The Drugged Balloonist* (1943; cat. no. 9), an intricate work unique in his oeuvre incorporating leaves, insect wings, handmade paper, magazine cutouts and poured paint.[16] Within days of the exhibition's opening it was purchased for $50 by the collector Saidie A. May, along with Motherwell's papier collé *The Joy of Living* (1943), and donated almost immediately to the Baltimore Museum of Art.[17] It was the first work that Baziotes had ever sold. Ethel later recalled the excitement. "It was a very dramatic sale. And it meant a lot to Peggy. Many thought the whole thing was like a toy for her, but this was someone taking her exhibition seriously."[18] Pollock's work, never formally identified, did not sell.[19]

The exhibition was received with mixed feelings, with many critics seemingly uncertain how to approach what was clearly an unfamiliar medium. "Paste, applied to waste, with taste," wrote one.[20] Among the supportive voices was that of Peggy's friend Jean Connolly, whose review mentioned Baziotes, Pollock and Reinhardt.[21]

Within days of the exhibition's close, the work of all three, in addition to that of Motherwell, was included in the gallery's next exhibition, the inaugural "Spring Salon for Young Artists." Again based on an idea originally conceived for Guggenheim Jeune, this time by Herbert Read, the show was largely organized by Howard Putzel.[22] Advertisements were placed in newspapers and periodicals, inviting artists under thirty-five years of age to bring "abstract and fantastic paintings and sculpture" to the gallery by 11 May for review by a jury.[23] In the absence of Breton and both Max and Jimmy Ernst, all of whom had served on the gallery's first jury — convened on Christmas Eve 1942 to select artists for the "Exhibition by 31 Women" — Piet Mondrian joined Duchamp, James Thrall Soby, James Johnson Sweeney, Putzel and Peggy to complete a group de-

scribed in the exhibition's press release as "two painters, two critics and two amateurs."[24] A points system was used, with each work attributed a score by each juror of between zero and ten. A minimum score of thirty was required for a work to be included.[25]

Thirty-three artists were selected, Baziotes among them. Others included Virginia Admiral, Busa, Kamrowski, Ibram Lassaw, Matta, Motherwell, I. Rice Pereira, Pollock, Reinhardt, and Hedda Sterne. The majority were represented by a single work, with prices ranging from $25 to $1000. Baziotes was one of a handful to show two, the paintings *The Mirror at Midnight I* and *II* (circa 1942; cat. no. 7) which he had completed the previous year. He also assisted Pollock in selecting a work for submission to the jury. Visiting his studio with Motherwell, they suggested *Stenographic Figure* (circa 1942, later acquired by MoMA) then titled simply *Painting*. Its subsequent presentation to the jury led to the now famous exchange in which Mondrian convinced an apparently disparaging Peggy of the painting's (and the artist's) merit.[26]

Notwithstanding the exhibition's duration — at thirty-nine days, it was the longest show held at Art of This Century — the gallery's financial report lists few sales.[27] Prominent among them, however, are both paintings by Baziotes, sold for $150 each. One appears to have been purchased by Peggy herself.[28] Indeed, it appears that of all the young artists to whom she had given an opportunity to exhibit in these first two exhibitions, it was Baziotes, along with Pollock, who had most caught her eye.

During the summer that followed, she sought to formalize the gallery's relationship with both artists. In July, Pollock received the first of three contracts that would run consecutively until the gallery's close in 1947. At around the same time, Baziotes received a card from Howard Putzel. "If you're back I'd like to come up with Peggy and see your work on Sunday afternoon at 4.30. Unless you've become a very bad artist you'll be asked to exhibit here and have us act as your dealer. Do phone if you're in town. Love to Ethel."[29] A short time later Peggy and Putzel visited Baziotes' studio, principally to discuss the idea of a first solo exhibition at the gallery. They found him depressed and unable to work. He told them that he planned to leave New York to spend the sum-

5
Exhibition
announcement,
"Paintings and
Drawings by
Baziotes," 1944,
designed by Jimmy
Ernst

3
William Baziotes,
Gerome Kamrowski,
and Jackson
Pollock
*Collaborative
Painting*, 1940–41
Oil and enamel
on canvas,
19 1/4 x 25 1/2 in
Collection of Mary
Jane Kamrowski

mer in his hometown of Reading, Pennsylvania. As a gesture of encouragement, and in an effort to alleviate any immediate financial troubles that he might be facing, Peggy purchased a small number of works. They included three large gouaches and a small oil, the identity of which are unknown, at a combined price of $450.[30] Peggy's support did not stop there, as Ethel later recalled. "The next week she sent Bill a wool robe and a navy blue Palm Beach suit that had belonged to her son, Sindbad."[31]

Late that summer, Putzel wrote again to see if Baziotes had returned. "Are you back in town? I'm most anxious to see what you've done. If you are back, may I come over on Wednesday evening? I'm at the gallery daily […] Lots of preparatory work for the season."[32] He had returned, but remained unsettled and had struggled to produce any work. He painted only a few hours at a time and then with great difficulty. Ethel attributed her husband's difficulties to the malnutrition and poor living conditions he experienced during the Depression, as a result of his family's impoverished situation.[33] "Peggy expected a show," he later recalled, "and I didn't have

one. Felt very obliged, but couldn't force. I had my terrible excuses, stopped going around so much."[34] An advertisement in the December 1943 issue of *View* magazine announcing Baziotes' début exhibition proved premature.[35] It was clear that the show Peggy and Putzel had envisaged for that year would have to be postponed.

They continued, however, to involve him in gallery activities. In December 1943, shortly after the opening of Pollock's début one-man exhibition, Baziotes' work was included in "Natural, Insane, Surrealist Art," a show of small-scale work organized to coincide with the Christmas season. Conceived by Ladislas Segy, a collector, dealer and authority on African art, the exhibition sought to instigate a dialogue between, on the one hand, natural objects and art by mentally insane patients, and on the other, Surrealist works by European and American artists.[36] The natural objects on display included skeletons, pieces of driftwood, and petrified tree roots. Shown alongside them were a series of drawings loaned from the collections of Segy and Max Ernst, several of which had been done by inmates of various Euro-

A 30 WEST FIFTY-SEVENTH STREET C

pean
Euro
Miró
inclu
nell,
show
B
brief
5 in
et w
em
Bau
ted
"Spr
trov
the
It w
with
artis
ral,
join
Ric
bef
cha
and
(19

40

42

Baziotes agreed to the dates, and set to work on final preparations. An announcement card for the exhibition was designed by Jimmy Ernst (fig. 5), while a press release seeking to explain the painter's work and approach was issued by the gallery shortly before the exhibition's opening. "His persistent search for a stronger self-expression has developed him into a creative artist. The slashing power in his paintings is not a brutal one. It is rather a strong force that gathered into color and form those everyday values and mysteries that concern all of us but which invariably get lost when they encounter realism. Baziotes' concept therefore rules out the use of accepted form and representation."[48]

In the last days of September, as Peggy and her new assistant Marius Bewley prepared for the opening of Art of This Century's third season, Baziotes brought his works to the gallery. With the help of Robert Motherwell, he began nervously to hang the show in both rooms of the north-facing Daylight Gallery. "We were both frightened and green," Motherwell later recalled. "I remember his turning white at a certain moment and saying, 'Bob, if you think this show is a mistake, that it's really not painting, I'd rather take it down right now before this thing goes through,' and my patting him on the back and saying, 'Come on, it's wonderful,' but really in my heart just as doubtful as he was."[49] Baziotes himself described the feeling as "very odd indeed." It was, according to Ethel, "the blind leading the blind, an overpowering adventure in which both of them were in over their heads."[50] Baziotes was thirty-two years old, Motherwell just twenty-nine.

The exhibition opened on 3 October 1944, and presented twenty-four works, including at least four gouaches and the collage from Baltimore. Two of the works – a painting, *Three Doors* (1944, Tel Aviv Museum of Art; cat. no. 12), and an untitled gouache (1943; cat. no. 10) — were listed as belonging to Peggy, and must have been acquired as part of her purchases in the year prior to the exhibition.[51] In addition to the collage, two other works had previously been shown at the gallery: *The Mirror at Midnight* (circa 1942), in the first Spring Salon, and *The Balcony*, in the second.[52] Prices for the works ranged from $25 to $200.

Baziotes would have been heartened by the warm response of critics and collectors. The financial reports for 1944 and 1945 list no fewer than twelve sales. Six were gouaches, indicating perhaps that more were included in the exhibition than were indicated on the checklist. Buyers included Bewley; Leo Castelli, the collector and gallerist; Milton Gendel, a Motherwell's fellow student at Columbia and for many years the Italian correspondent for *Art News*; Maria Motherwell, the young Mexican actress wife of Robert; Lois Orswell, the pioneering Connecticut collector who would later donate this, and many other works, to the Fogg Art Museum; and Sam A. Lewisohn, the New York collector. Paintings were purchased by Rudi Blesh, the author, critic and connoisseur of jazz music, Thomas B. Hess, the future editor of *Art News* (*The Hourglass*, circa 1944; cat. no. 16);[53] Wright Ludington, the collector and philanthropist, at the time serving in the US military (*The Balcony*, circa 1944; fig. 5 in Michael Preble's essay in this catalogue)[54]; Douglas McAgy, then curator of the San Francisco Museum of Art; and Bernard Reis, the gallery'accountant and father of the artist Barbara (*The Boudoir*, 1944; fig. 6). *The Schoolroom* (1943; cat. no. 11) was purchased some years later by Clement Greenberg. Another, unidentified work appears to have been bought by the brother of Sidney Janis. In a letter postmarked 31 October 1944, Janis enclosed a check for "the small painting" his brother had purchased. "As I know he's good for it I'll wait rather than have you do so."[55]

Baziotes was understandably taken aback by the reception of his work: "Underestimated interest of public. Not a hard-luck pioneer. Strange, most astonishing people would come and buy. Very exciting period. Fantastic. Leading a lonely life, no connection with world, thrown, thrust into it suddenly."

The reception of critics was, on the whole, similarly favorable. The first review, published a day before the opening and for which a number of works had been arranged in the gallery before the show had been hung, came from Maude Riley. After a lukewarm beginning — "a full-length view of the painter Baziotes, seen on occasions in company of other young men shown tentatively by the gallery" — her tone improved as she took a particular interest in the smaller gouaches. "The color contained in them is of boundless wealth. They appear spontaneously de-

6
William Baziotes,
The Boudoir, 1944
Oil on canvas,
34 1/2 x 50 in
Private collection,
Los Angeles

signed and painted in a fever of inspired intent. Framed and exhibited, they should in themselves account most impressively for the interest the artist has incited in himself and his work."[56] Edward Alden Jewell, writing in *The New York Times*, was less certain. "I suppose he should not be called non-objective, because there are naturalistic titles. Make of this liaison what you can."[57] Baziotes himself later recognized that Jewell "didn't know what the hell to make of me."[58]

The most thorough and insightful review came, somewhat inevitably, from Greenberg. "All credit is due to Peggy Guggenheim for her enterprise in presenting young and unrecognized artists at her Art of This Century gallery. But even more to her credit is her acumen. Two of the abstract painters she has recently introduced — Jackson Pollock and William Baziotes — reveal more than promise: on the strength of their first one-man shows they have already placed themselves among the six or seven best painters we possess. Baziotes, whose show closed last month, is unadulterated talent, natural painter and all painter. He issues in a single jet, deflected by nothing extraneous to painting. Two or three of his larger oils may become masterpieces in several years, once they stop

disturbing us by their nervousness, by their unexampled color — off-shades in the intervals between red and blue, red and yellow, yellow and green, all depth, involution, and glow — and by their very originality. Baziotes' gouaches had their own proper quality, which is the intensity of their whites and higher colors."[59]

Three days later it was the turn of Motherwell, whose début exhibition included almost fifty paintings, drawings, collages and papiers collés. Baziotes returned the favor, helping his friend with the show's hanging (figs. 7, 8). Greenberg took the opportunity to compare the two artists, and in doing so laid a heavy burden of expectation on their young shoulders. "Motherwell is a more finished but less intense painter than Baziotes, less upsetting because more traditional and easier to take. One is Dionysian and the other Apollonian [...]" It was clear, he went on, that "the future of American painting depends on what [Motherwell], Baziotes, Pollock, and only a comparatively few others do from now on."[60]

The momentum afforded by his exposure at Art of This Century continued with Baziotes' inclusion in two important New York group shows before the year was out. The first, "Abstract and Surrealist Art

7
William Baziotes seated on a Correalist rocker, installing "Robert Motherwell 1944: Paintings, Papiers collés, Drawings," Art of This Century, photographed by Manny Farber, New York, October 1944

8
William Baziotes installing "Robert Motherwell 1944: Paintings, Papiers collés, Drawings," Art of This Century, photographed by Manny Farber, New York, October 1944

44

in America" at the Mortimer Brandt Gallery, accompanied the publication of Janis' book of the same name.[61] The second, "Forty American Moderns," was mounted by Putzel at his 67 Gallery, and included work by a roll call of artists — Calder, Cornell, Adolph Gottlieb, Hare, Hans Hofmann, Motherwell, Pereira, Pollock, Rothko, Seliger, Dorothea Tanning, and Mark Tobey among them — whose future successes say much for Putzel's prescience.[62] Later the same month, while a small number of his gouaches and paintings were included in an informal exhibition of "Christmas suggestions" at Art of This Century, an advertisement placed by Peggy in *View* magazine proudly promoted the gallery as "agents for Motherwell, Baziotes, David Hare [...]"[63] Within the space of six busy months, Baziotes' careeer had turned around.

At Motherwell's prompting, it was soon afforded a precious security. The two artists enjoyed a close friendship. Although younger, Motherwell was well traveled and closer to New York's Surrealist *milieu*, and took it upon himself to guide his friend's development. The previous year, less than a month before Baziotes' show opened, Motherwell had spoken honestly about his situation. "For you, as for me, there are only two possible courses: to go to France forever [...] or remain here and be psycho-analyzed. If you are going to do the first, you ought to do certain things, from a strategic point of view — which I will tell you about when I see you. I love your instinctiveness and emotionalism, but at the same time you need someone to make a map for you occasionally & steadily. Matta used to do it for me when I was filled with instinct, but now I begin to see the whole terrain. And I beg you to break with the young Surrealists — David [Hare], Michel, Catherine [Yarrow?], [Isamu] Noguchi, Jacqueline [Lamba] & the whole crowd — they can only confuse you, and they are cynical, ignorant and sterile. If I did not greatly care about you, I would say nothing, but one of the things you least understand — if I may say so — is how to make your energy productive, and one of the chief ways of doing this is to remain *only* in milieus which make you *want* to paint [...] I don't mean, be rude — just stay away. Otherwise you remain confused. Please excuse me for this lecture, but with your talent & good will it is shameful that you rest in your present state, and I think it has more to do with the people you see than anything else [...]"[64]

Early in 1945, Motherwell again sought to act in Baziotes' interests. "I told a man about you who might give you a contract if you want it — though I don't know how good the offer is. Anyhow, I spoke to Peggy about it, and she talks as though she is going to give up her gallery after this season, and as if it is up to us to fend for ourselves."[65] The "man" in question was Samuel Kootz, who was beginning to gather a stable of artists that would eventually include a number of Peggy's artists.[66] He offered both artists $200 a month in return for their complete annual output, set at a minimum of seventy-five paintings and drawings.

It had been apparent for some time that Peggy did not plan to stay long in New York. Ethel Baziotes described her as "disenchanted," and as having "a predilection for Europe."[67] As it turned out, she would stay until the early summer of 1947, but the uncertainty was enough to convince both Baziotes and Motherwell to accept Kootz's offer. In mid-February both artists signed contracts. David Porter, who had

recently selected Baziotes' work for inclusion in the groundbreaking exhibition "Personal Statement: Painting Prophecy 1950," lost no time in writing to Grace McCann Morley, director of the San Francisco Museum of Art, with the news. "Peggy told me today that San [sic] Kootz had agreed to give Baziotes $200 a month in return for handling his work. Too bad for Miss Guggenheim, she has lost a talented young artist."[68]

Despite his defection, it seems that Peggy kept a small stock of Baziotes' work at Art of This Century. Indeed several months later he was among twenty-nine artists included in the gallery's 1945 Autumn Salon. It was, however, the last time that he would show there. Along with Hare, Motherwell, Pollock and Seliger, he had been one of Peggy's greatest discoveries, and played a significant role in ensuring that her gallery would achieve its stated ambition to serve the future, rather than the past. She, in turn, had thrust this young and determined painter into the sights of critics, curators, and collectors across the United States. The fight had been won and the search of William Baziotes moved on.

45

This essay develops a shorter text by the author regarding William Baziotes' début one-man exhibition at Art of This Century included in the essay "Serving the Future - The Exhibitions at Art of This Century, 1942–47," written for the book *Peggy Guggenheim and Frederick Kiesler. The Story of Art of This Century*, edited by S. Davidson and P. Rylands, New York, The Solomon R. Guggenhiem Foundation, 2004, pp. 284–359.

[1] Jimmy Ernst to William Baziotes, 14 April 1942, William and Ethel Baziotes Papers, 1916-1992, Archives of American Art (Smithsonian Institution, Washington, D.C.), microfilm N 70-21: 107. The gallery to which Ernst refers was part of the E. Weyhe bookshop at 794 Lexington Avenue, New York.

[2] André Breton to William Baziotes, postmarked 7 September 1942, William and Ethel Baziotes Papers… cit., microfilm N 70-21: 116. The list included other Americans — Alexander Calder, Joseph Cornell, Morris Hirshfield — in addition to Jimmy Ernst.

[3] The exhibition ran 14 October–7 November 1942.

[4] Press Release for Art of This Century, n.d. (circa 20 October 1942), New York Public Library Pamphlet Box, Archives of American Art (Smithsonian Institution, Washington, D.C.), microfilm N 429: 159–60.

[5] Ethel Baziotes, conversation with the author, New York, 13 February 2004.

[6] It was during one such evening that Ethel first met Mondrian, an artist much admired by her husband: "He was like a priest, like his work. He said to me, 'you and I are the quietest people here.'" Ethel Baziotes, conversation with the author, New York City, 13 February 2004.

[7] Baziotes, Pollock and Kamrowski had first experimented with automatist techniques in the latter's studio during the winter of 1940–41.

[8] Robert Motherwell, letter to James T. Valliere, 31 August 1964, Jackson Pollock Papers, Archives of American Art (Smithsonian Institution, Washington, D.C.). Peter Busa and his future wife Jeanne Juell, and Matta and Ann Clark are also known to have been involved on different occasions.

[9] *Ibidem*.

[10] Press release for Art of This Century, n.d. (circa 20 October 1942) cit. Putzel's arrival followed the departure of Jimmy Ernst. Soon afterwards, Ernst opened the Norlyst Gallery at 59 West 56th Street.

[11] "Exhibition of Collages, Papiers-collés, and Photo-montages," 4–26 November 1938, Guggenheim Jeune, London.

[12] Press clipping, Art of This Century scrapbook, Peggy Guggenheim Papers, Solomon R. Guggenheim Foundation, New York (portions are duplicated as Printed Material relating to Guggenheim Jeune and Art of This Century galleries, 1938–1946, Archives of American Art, Smithsonian Institution, Washington, D.C.).

[13] The exhibition ran from 16 April–15 May 1943. Robert Mattison has estimated that in 1943 there were fewer than twenty collages in New York between MoMA, the Gallatin collection, and Art of This Century. R. Saltonstall Mattison, *Robert Motherwell – The Formative Years*, Ann Arbor, UMI Press, 1986–87, p. 77.

[14] Several reviews suggest that the earliest work was dated 1911. Loans included Ernst's *The Hat Makes The Man* (1920, MoMA) and George Grosz's *Remember Uncle August, the Unhappy Inventor* (1919, since acquired by the Musée National d'Art Moderne, Centre Georges Pompidou, Paris). Ernst showed several of his *Semaine de Bonté* collages, then owned by Peggy: see *Art of This Century; Objects-Drawings-Photographs-Paintings-Sculpture-Collages, 1910-1942*, edited by P. Guggenheim, New York, Art Aid Co., 1942, p. 149. Several other works — those of Arp, Gris, Picasso and Schwitters, for example — were most likely also borrowed from the gallery's permanent collection.

[15] Robert Motherwell, letter to James T. Valliere, 31 August 1964, Jackson Pollock Papers cit.

[16] Motherwell, who would devote much of his subsequent career to the medium, compared his first experiences of the medium with "making beautiful love for the first time." Robert Motherwell, filmed interview shown during an exhibition at the Solomon R. Guggenheim Museum, New York, 1985.

[17] Donald Paneth's *William Baziotes: A Literary Portrait*, based on a 1952 interview with the artist, states that the works were purchased two days after the opening. D. Paneth, *William Baziotes: A Literary Portrait*, unpublished manuscript, William and Ethel Baziotes Papers… cit.

[18] Ethel Baziotes, conversation with the author, New York City, 13 February 2004.

[19] Motherwell believed that Pollock destroyed his work shortly thereafter. Robert Motherwell, interview conducted by Sidney Simon in New York in January 1967, "Concerning the Beginnings of the New York School 1939–1943," *Art International*, 11, summer 1967, p. 22. The artist's *catalogue raisonné* lists three collages (nos. 1023–25) of around 1943. One of these may be the work submitted to this exhibition. F.V. O'Connor, E.V. Thaw, *Jackson Pollock: A Catalogue Raisonné of Paintings, Drawings and Other Works*, vol. IV, New Haven-London, Yale University Press, 1978.

[20] "Art About Town," *Brooklyn Eagle*, 2 May 1943.

[21] J. Connolly, "Exhibition of Collage," *The Nation*, 156, 1 May 1943, p. 643. Connolly had assumed responsibility for Clement Greeenberg's column in *The Nation* while he was serving in the army.

[22] The original idea of a Spring salon for young artists had been proposed by Read in early 1939. Like Peggy's broader plan to found a museum of modern art in London, the initiative was thwarted by the outbreak of World War II.

[23] *The New York Times*, 1 May 1943. The notice carried by *Art News* gave the date of 8 May. "The Last Word," *Art News*, 42, 1–14 May 1943, p. 7.

[24] Exhibition press release, Peggy Guggenheim Papers cit. In her memoirs, Peggy also listed Alfred H. Barr, Jr. among the jurors. It is conceivable that he was added after the issue of the press release or that she was confusing the 1943 Salon jury with that of 1944. P. Guggenheim, *Out of This Century: Confessions of an Art Addict*, New York, Universe Books, 1979, p. 284. Soby recalled that the jurors would sit in the gallery while Putzel — "a born assasin of works of art" — carried works to and from the storeroom. J. Thrall Soby, *My Life in the Art World*, unpublished manuscript, Museum of Modern Art Archives, Soby Papers, Add VI, box 66a.

[25] "From None to Ten," *Art Digest*, 17, 15 May 1943, p. 8. Among those whose work was rejected was the seventeen year-old painter Charles Seliger. He did, however, receive encouragement from Putzel, and would go on to show at both Putzel's 67 Gallery and Jimmy Ernst's Norlyst Gallery before returning to Art of This Century for the Autumn Salon and a one-man exhibition in 1945.

[26] See J. Ernst, *A Not-So-Still Life: A Memoir*, New York, St. Martin's / Marek, 1984, pp. 241–42, and S. Naifeh, G. White Smith, *Jackson Pollock: An American Saga*, New York, Clarkson N. Potter, 1989, pp. 444–46.

[27] The exhibition ran 18 May–26 June 1943. Bernard and Rebecca Reis Papers Research Library Special Collections & Visual Resources, The Getty Institute, Los Angeles (portions are duplicated as the Bernard J. Reis Papers, 1934-1979, Archives of American Art, Smithsonian Institution, Washington, D.C.).

[28] Exactly when they were sold is not entirely clear. It is known that Rudi Blesh purchased two works, including *The Mirror at Midnight I*, in 1945, and kept the work until his death in 1985. The 1942–43 financial report lists *The Mirror at Midnight* (whether *I* or *II* is not known) as a handwritten addition to Peggy's own collection. It is again listed in the 1944 report, but absent from that of 1945, suggesting that it was sold. It is unclear whether this is the second version, or that acquired the same year by Blesh.

[29] Howard Putzel to William Baziotes, undated postcard (presumed summer 1943), William and Ethel Baziotes Papers… cit., microfilm N 70-21: 115.

[30] D. Paneth, *op. cit.*

[31] Ethel Baziotes, quoted in V.M. Dortch, *Peggy Guggenheim and Her Friends*, Milan, Berenice Art Books, 1994, p. 104.

[32] Howard Putzel to William Baziotes, dated "Thursday", "September 16th, 1943" (handwritten later addition), William and

Ethel Baziotes Papers… cit., microfilm N 70-21: 108.

[33] *Flying Tigers: Painting and Sculpture in New York 1939-1946*, exhibition catalogue, Providence, Rhode Island, Bell Gallery, Brown University, 1985, p. 5.

[34] D. Paneth, *op. cit.*

[35] *View*, series III, no. 4, December 1943, inside cover.

[36] The exhibition ran 1–31 Decemebr 1943. Segy's involvement is noted in one review. D. Gilbert, "Surrealist Exhibit Turns Psychiatric," *New York World-Telegram*, 14 December 1943. Peggy later suggested to Melvin Lader that Marcel Duchamp may have proposed the idea. Peggy Guggenheim, interview with Melvin Lader, 3 April 1978, quoted in M.P. Lader, *Peggy Guggenheim Art of This Century: The Surrealist Milieu and the American Avant-Garde, 1942-1947*, Ph.D. Art History Dissertation, University of Delaware, Newark, June 1981, p. 254, n. 27.

[37] "Green background, slight suggestion of forms, great many heavy lines running through it. Flesh in it, but not a sensation picture. Understatement. Spiritually have an effect of Baudelaire's poem 'The Balcony,'" D. Paneth, *op. cit.*

[38] This list of jurors — Barr, Duchamp, Soby, Sweeney, Peggy and Putzel — appeared in *Art Digest*. "Calling Young Surrealists," *Art Digest*, 18, 1 April 1944, p. 26. Barr had been added since the first Spring Salon in 1943. Kenneth Macpherson was later added, and is listed in *The New York Times* review. E. Alden Jewell, "Peggy Guggenheim Opens Art Show," *The New York Times*, 10 May 1944. The exhibition ran 2 May–3 June 1944.

[39] C. Greenberg, "Art," *The Nation*, 158, 27 May 1944, p. 634.

[40] Sidney Janis to William Baziotes, 20 April 1944, William and Ethel Baziotes Papers… cit., microfilm N 70-21: 128.

[41] Sidney Janis to William Baziotes, undated card, William and Ethel Baziotes Papers… cit., microfilm N 70-21: 130.

[42] William and Ethel Baziotes Papers… cit., microfilm N 70-21: 47. S. Janis, *Abstract and Surrealist Art in America*, New York, Reynal and Hitchcock, 1944, p. 101. The statement was widely reproduced in subsequent publications, including the exhibition catalogue for David Porter's 1945 exhibition "Personal Statement: A Painting Prophecy 1950."

[43] D. Paneth, *op. cit.*

[44] Ethel Baziotes, conversation with the author, New York City, 13 February 2004. It is not known what was purchased. In D. Paneth, *op. cit.* Baziotes says "some more, for $500."

[45] *Ibidem*.

[46] Clement Greenberg to William Baziotes, 23 August 1944, William and Ethel Baziotes Papers… cit., microfilm N 70-21: 111.

[47] Peggy Guggenheim to William Baziotes, William and Ethel Baziotes Papers… cit., microfilm N 70-21: 145.

[48] "Baziotes Has First One-Man Show,"

William and Ethel Baziotes Papers… cit. The identity of its author is unclear. Lader suggests that it could have been either Putzel or Sweeney. M.P. Lader, *op. cit.*, pp. 263–64.

[49] Robert Motherwell, interview with John Jones, New York City, 25 October 1965, Archives of American Art (Smithsonian Institution, Washington, D.C.).

[50] Ethel Baziotes, conversation with the author, New York City, 13 February 2004.

[51] *Three Doors* was one of thirty-six works by European and American artists donated by Peggy Guggenheim to the Tel Aviv Museum of Art in 1954–55.

[52] It is unclear whether the work listed as *The Mirror at Midnight* was the first or second version. Both had been included in the 1943 Spring Salon.

[53] D. Paneth, *op. cit.* The news came in a letter from Peggy. "Dear Bill, I just sold the Hour Glass for $150 to a Lt. Hess, charming young aviator. Also the Wittenborns are coming up to your house to look at your new work if you have anything. They have been fussing for three months and can't decide between all of yours and two of Bobs." Peggy Guggenheim to William Baziotes, 26 January 1945, William and Ethel Baziotes Papers… cit., microfilm N 70-21: 147. Hess had been an assistant to Alfred H. Barr, Jr. and Dorothy Miller at MoMA during 1942 before joining the U.S. Army Air Force. The Wittenborns were renowned New York art booksellers, with whom Motherwell collaborated on a series of books entitled *Documents of Modern Art*. See card from Wittenborns to Baziotes in xeroxes, frame 112. "Bob" Motherwell's exhibition followed that of Baziotes.

[54] Ludington's purchase, like those of Blesh, was made in 1945, the year after the exhibition had closed. It is mentioned in a letter to Baziotes from Robert Motherwell. "I had a letter from Peggy yesterday, and she says she sold The Balcony to Wright Ludington and 2 gouaches, so I think you might go around and get the money […] It's awfully good news about your sales." Robert Motherwell to William Baziotes, 6 May 1945, William and Ethel Baziotes Papers… cit., microfilm N 70-21: 140.

[55] Sidney Janis to William Baziotes, 31 October 1944 (postmark), William and Ethel Baziotes Papers… cit., microfilm N 70-21: 131.

[56] M. Riley, "Baziotes' Color," *Art Digest*, 19, 1 October 1944, p. 12. Peggy had written to Baziotes a few days before the exhibition opened to notify him of Riley's visit. "Could you please send me some paintings by next Monday, so that Art Digest can write about them in their next issue which has to print next Wed." Peggy Guggenheim to William Baziotes, dated "Tuesday," William and Ethel Baziotes Papers… cit., microfilm N 70-21.

[57] E. Alden Jewell, "Art: A Hectic Week," *The New York Times*, 8 October 1944.

[58] D. Paneth, *op. cit.*

[59] C. Greenberg, "Art," *The Nation*, 159, 11 November 1944, p. 598.

[60] *Ibidem*, p. 599.

[61] The exhibition ran 29 November–30 December 1944. It had previously been shown as "Abstract and Surrealist Art in the United States" in Cincinnati, Denver, Seattle, Santa Barbara and San Francisco.

[62] The exhibition ran 4–30 December 1944.

[63] *View*, series IV, no. 4, December 1944, p. 109.

[64] Robert Motherwell to William Baziotes, 6 September 1944, William and Ethel Baziotes Papers… cit., microfilm N 70-21: 0139.

[65] Robert Motherwell to William Baziotes, n.d., William and Ethel Baziotes Papers… cit., microfilm N 70-21: 141.

[66] David Hare and Hans Hofmann were also later represented following exhibitions at Art of This Century.

[67] Ethel Baziotes, conversation with the author, New York City, 13 February 2004.

[68] David Porter to Grace McCann Morley, 18 February 1945, David Porter Papers, Archives of American Art (Smithsonian Institution, Washington, D.C.). The exhibition was held at Porter's Washington, D.C. gallery in February 1945.

To the House of Psyche and Amor —

"We are all fragments walking amongst
fragments"

— Nietzsche

— the poetry of Nerves
the Drama of the Nervous System

"Mother of Memories
Mistress of Mistresses"

— The Balcony
Baudelaire

"Give a good bull"

"Lincoln was a poet"

"There is an unconscious collaboration amongst artists"

"For a hundred mistakes — if I find one thing..."

"I always want to be a hungry fighter"

— The wedding of the umbrella and the
sewing machine

May I leave you with this fragment from Baziotes'
Notes?

"—Hokusai began his day by washing his paint brushes"

On the Occasion of the Venice Exhibition
of the Art of William Baziotes

Ethel Baziotes, July 2004

To the House of Psyche and Amor —

"We are all fragments walking amongst
fragments."
— Nietzche

— The poetry of Nerves
    The Drama of the Nervous System

"Mother of Memories
Mistress of Mistresses"
— The Balcony
    Baudelaire

— The wedding of the umbrella and
    the sewing machine

"Give me a good bull"

"Lincoln was a poet"

"There is an unconscious collaboration amongst
artists"

"For a hundred mistakes — if I find one thing…"

"I always want to be a hungry fighter"

May I leave you with this fragment from Baziotes'
notes?

— "Hokusai began his day by washing his paint
brushes."

Ethel and William
Baziotes,
photographed
by Francis Lee,
circa 1947

49

Remembrance*

Jimmy Ernst

I felt most comfortable with Ethel and Bill Baziotes. I could talk to them easily and, from the very beginning, there was no doubt that both, but particularly Ethel, felt very protective of me. It was almost impossible to imagine them apart from each other. Just to watch them walk on a street, dressed like a proud working couple on a gray Sunday stroll, made it unmistakable that they were "one bone and one flesh," bonded for life and perhaps beyond. Ethel's Byzantine-icon face rarely lost its serenity other than her eyes widening in astonishment or her delicate lips pursing as if to prepare the Madonna for a broad smile. If her laughter was decorous, Bill's usually somber and quizzical mien, that of a truck driver intent on the road, transformed itself into a simultaneous stretching of all facial muscles to the sound of bellringing laughter. He seemed a curious mixture interchangeable of earthiness and sophistication. He held his head as if the collar of his shirt were starched and high. His rugged face would not have been out of place in the Greek village of his ancestors. His friends could not avoid comparing him to a somewhat smaller Humphrey Bogart, a hat securely on his head, a cigarette dangling from the side of his mouth, one hand, as through always ready, defiantly protecting itself in the overcoat pocket. What did not fit the image was a slightly bulbous nose and the inevitable umbrella he seemed to hold at the ready against any kind of weather, even indoors [...]

Baziotes, whom I knew best, was a living example of an American, who, unlike his European counterparts, had become an artist without growing up in the shadow of Greek, Roman, Gothic or Baroque edifices. His landscape, and that of other Americans, was silhouetted by coal-mine lift cages, oil derricks and grain silos, skyscrapers, New England church spires and water towers. The land ebbed and flowed into endless plains delineated by mighty rivers, infinite forests and wilderness. With all that, Bill was exploring the interior of yet another landscape in his small room. He was giving life to dreams and to intuitive suppositions of what lay hidden in the secret and locked rooms of nature. His were visions alluding to recognizable imagery that transformed themselves into mythological apparitions from a pantheon of gnomes, serpents and birds. Spontaneous and thorny meanderings of the brush clustered into a clearly intended sensuality. Soft pink of flesh swam into vision as the fragment of a nude obliquely observed in a mirror. His Venus, as he once told me, was at her most glowing and erotic "when I watch her straightening the bedcovers after making love."

* Excerpts from J. Ernst, *A Not-So-Still Life*, Wainscott, New York, Pushcart Press, 1984/1992, pp. 186–89.

Remembering William Baziotes

Charles Seliger, 5 March 2004

In 1945, at the age of nineteen, I had my first one-person exhibition at Peggy Guggenheim's Art of This Century. I found myself in the company of Jackson Pollock, Mark Rothko and William Baziotes, who would eventually receive recognition for being the important innovators of a new direction in art, when Abstract Expressionism emerged as the most important post-war art movement. I had the opportunity to be part of this exciting new spirit in American art that would have world-wide influence. I was especially fascinated by the lyricism of Baziotes' biomorphic paintings. His work revealed a personal response to the myriad organic images found in nature. He fused his love of poetry and painting into a statement combining form and color into dream-like revelations of nature's secrets. He was the poet of the Abstract Expressionist movement. About 1945, I met Bill for the first time, and later became a friend. My shyness held me back from intruding on his privacy, which I now regret. Ethel has since chided me about not visiting them more often, as I would have been welcome. Bill's pretense of toughness hid his easy going, down to earth attitude, his sensitivity and vulnerability. I remember him vividly, his suave, urbane manner, his humor, the slick black hair and the cigarette dangling from his lips, well dressed, with that mysterious intensity that one associated with film noir movies of the time.

Seeing Bill and Ethel together was seeing an exotic, lovely woman with beautiful long hair, wearing wonderful colors, extremely pleasant, quiet, somewhat elusive and deeply devoted to her husband. I remember, one time, visiting them at a gathering of artists and friends at their home. Bill with his mischievous smile was seated, I seem to recall, on either a ladder or back of a chair. That evening he showed his empathy for my being so young and new to the art scene. Looking over at me and in a very clear voice, "You are 19, how come you are not influenced by any of us, it amazes me." This said so all could hear. I guess he knew a generous pat on the back would be welcome and he generously gave it. A somewhat similar moment occurred at the 1951 exhibition of American Abstract Art at MoMA. I was in the elevator, standing next to Jackson Pollock with Bill and others. Bill was across from us, with that sly smile and twinkle in his eye, he joked, "Charlie, you better move away from Jackson, or you will be influenced by him". Pollock responded, "Maybe he will influence me". I knew about Bill's love of poetry and that he was a voracious reader. What I found so meaningful to me was the diversity of writers he read. Three, at least, that I was also reading, and how I wish now that we had discussed them. Jacob Wassermann's *World's Illusion*, a dense, richly detailed novel of the lives of intense, complex people. I do not imagine many of the other artists I knew ever read Wassermann. Then there was Bill's interest in the writing of the French entomologist, J. Henri Fabre, who wrote lyrically about insect life. Paul Valéry, whose work he read earlier than I, but who I continue to read with ever renewed interest. Bill successfully distilled all of his reading into the luminous, timeless beauty of his canvases. He was a unique and deeply personal artist.

As I am writing this and recalling Bill Baziotes, somehow the actor John Garfield comes to mind, small of stature, handsome, serious, intense, yet humorous. I think of both, who left us too soon and at their peak.

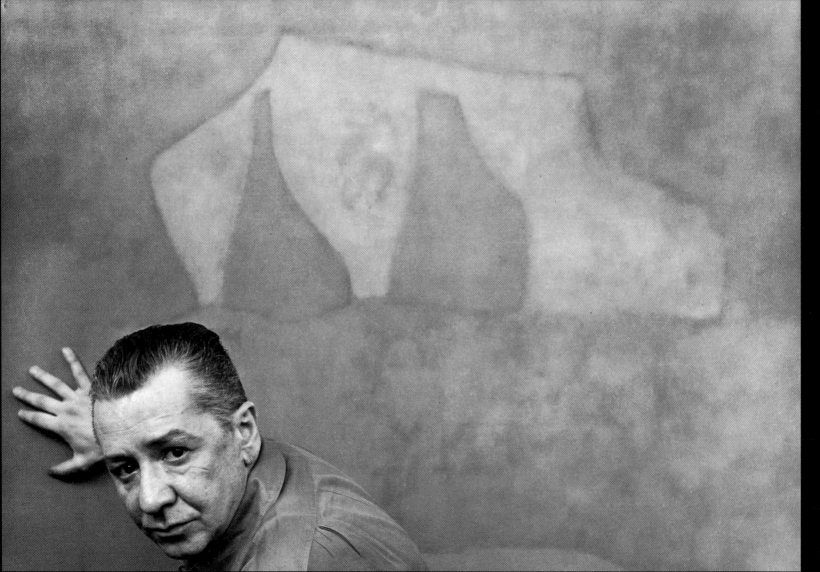

Catalogue of the Works

Notes on an Auction of a Collection

"Important Twentieth Century Unreserved Art Auction of Recently Discovered Works by William Baziotes (1912-1963) from the Private Collection of Constance & The Late Harry Baziotes (Held September 25, 1999 in Reading, Pennsylvania by Pennypacker-Andrews Auction Centre, Inc. of Shillington, Pennsylvania)."

My first knowledge of this event was in September 2003, when I saw the auction catalogue in the artist's file in the library of the National Gallery of Art in Washington, D.C. The catalogue detailed the sale of the collection of the artist's deceased brother and his wife. Of the 239 works offered, only 126 works were illustrated (30 in color, 96 in black and white).

If the illustrations present an overview, then the majority of works appear to date from the early 1930s, before Baziotes' Surrealist endeavors. The still lifes and figure studies were most likely done before and during his 1930s classes. There are a few, however, that show the influence of Dalí's particular brand of Surrealism. Others hint at more accomplished automatist works to come; and a few sketches allude to several post-1930s paintings.

An effort is being made to include several of the more finished and accomplished works in the upcoming catalogue raisonné, along with works that relate to finished paintings. None of these works are included in this exhibition.

To my knowledge, no museum curator or scholar familiar with Baziotes' work had the opportunity to encourage his brother's widow to seek a more studied approach to the disposal of this collection. Sadly, with the dispersal of this collection we have lost the ability to study these works, to compare them with other paintings and drawings. Shortly after my discovery of this sale, I began to see minor figure drawings, all unsigned, showing up at internet auctions.

William Baziotes Catalogue Raisonné

This exhibition marks the beginning of the William Baziotes catalogue raisonné project. Research has already begun with the objective to document all of the artist's paintings and works on paper.

This documentation will include title, date, media, size, inscriptions and images, where possible. Provenance, a record of the various owners of the work from creation to present, will also be researched.

In detailing provenance, it is understood that some owners may not wish to be identified by name. In such cases, their anonymity will be secure and the phrase "Private Collection" will be used.

Regrettably, a number of works sold through auctions are already lost — lost in the sense that the current owners do not respond to inquiries forwarded through auction houses. In this case, the work will be categorized as "Present Location Unknown."

This project will be announced to professionals — museum curators, gallery directors and collections — through advertising in popular art periodicals. A website will be constructed for the project and will allow for data entry and notations. Until that time, inquiries and information can be sent via email to my attention at baziotes@verizon.net.

Michael Preble

1
Untitled, 1934–36
Watercolor over graphite
on wove paper, 11 15/16 x 9 in
(30.32 x 22.86 cm)
Washington, D.C., National Gallery
of Art. Gift of Ethel Baziotes in honor
of Adlai E. Stevenson and Chief Joseph
of the Nez Perce 2004

2
Untitled, circa 1936–38
Watercolor, ink and graphite
on paper, 13 15/16 x 9 15/16 in
(35.40 x 25.24 cm)
Estate of William Baziotes

58

3
*Untitled (Self-Portrait
as a Clown)*, circa 1938
Oil on canvas, 28 x 20 in
(71.12 x 50.8 cm)
Estate of William Baziotes

60

4

Untitled, circa 1940s
Gouache on paper, 6 1/8 x 9 1/2 in
(15.56 x 24.13 cm)
Estate of William Baziotes

5
The Accordion of Flesh, circa 1941
Oil on canvas, 20 x 26 in
(50.8 x 66.4 cm)
Private collection

62

6
Leonardo da Vinci's Butterfly, 1942
Oil on canvas, 19 1/4 x 23 in
(50.17 x 58.42 cm)
Private collection

The Mirror at Midnight II, circa 1942
Oil on canvas, 20 1/8 x 28 1/8 in
(30.48 x 40.64 cm)
Courtesy Michael Rosenfeld Gallery,
New York

Untitled, circa 1942–43
Watercolor and chalk
on paper, 14 x 19 3/4 in
(35.56 x 50.10 cm)
Estate of William Baziotes

9

The Drugged Balloonist, 1943
Collage of printed paper, ink,
and graphite pencil on paperboard
18 1/4 x 24 in
(46.36 x 60.96 cm)
The Baltimore Museum of Art. Bequest
of Saidie A. May (BMA 1951.266)

66

10

Untitled, 1943
Gouache on black-wove paper
construction, 9 1/16 x 12 in
(23.02 x 30.48 cm)
Venice, Peggy Guggenheim Collection
(Solomon R. Guggenheim Foundation,
New York)

11
The Schoolroom, 1943
Oil on canvas, 15 3/4 x 19 in
(40.05 x 48.26 cm)
East Lansing, Michigan, Kresge Art
Museum, Michigan State University.
Gift of Clement Greenberg

12

Three Doors, 1944
Oil on canvas, 28 1/8 x 22 1/4 in
(71.5 x 56.5 cm)
Collection of the Tel Aviv Museum of
Art. Gift of Peggy Guggenheim, Venice,
through the America-Israel Cultural
Foundation, 1954

13

The Stage, 1944
Oil on canvas, 16 x 22 in
(40.64 x 55.88 cm)
Dr. and Mrs. Jerome Dersh

14
The Wine Glass, 1944
Duco on canvas, 26 1/4 x 20 1/4 in
(66.68 x 51.44 cm)
Estate of William Baziotes

72

15

The Parachutists, 1944
Duco enamel on canvas, 30 x 40 in
(76.2 x 101.6 cm)
Venice, Solomon R. Guggenheim
Foundation. Gift of Ethel Baziotes, 2004

The Hourglass, circa 1944
Oil on canvas, 30 x 24 in
(76.2 x 60.96 cm)
Mr. and Mrs. Meredith Long

74

17

The Room, 1945
Gouache on pressboard, 17 15/16 x 24 in
(45.56 x 60.96 cm)
Venice, Peggy Guggenheim Collection
(Solomon R. Guggenheim Foundation,
New York)

18
Still Life, 1945
Oil on canvas, 36 1/4 x 47 15/16 in
(92.08 x 121.76 cm)
St. Louis, Washington University
Gallery of Art. University Purchase,
Bixby Fund, 1946

19

Night Figure, No. 1, circa 1945
Watercolor, ink, gouache and pencil
on paper, 18 x 15 1/8 in
(45.72 x 38.42 cm)
New York, Solomon R. Guggenheim
Museum

20

The Web, 1946
Oil on canvas, 30 x 24 in
(76.2 x 60.96 cm)
Ithaca, New York, Herbert F. Johnson
Museum of Art, Cornell University.
Membership Purchase and David M.
Solinger (Class of 1926) Funds

78

21
Pierrot, 1947
Oil on canvas, 42 1/8 x 36 in
(106.99 x 91.44 cm)
Washington, D.C., National Gallery of
Art, Ailsa Mellon Bruce Fund 1984.43.1

22
Figures in Seascape, 1947
Watercolor, pen and ink
on paper, 12 x 18 in
(30.48 x 45.72 cm)
Collection of the Birmingham Museum
of Art, Alabama. Gift of Isadore Pizitz

23

Night Mirror, 1947
Oil on canvas, 48 7/16 x 59 13/16 in
(123.03 x 151.92 cm)
Poughkeepsie, New York, Francis
Lehman Loeb Art Center, Vassar College.
Gift of Mrs. John D. Rockefeller 3rd
(Blanchette Hooker, Class of 1931)

24

Water Form, 1947
Oil on canvas, 23 1/8 x 23 7/8 in
(50.8 x 60.6 cm)
Contemporary Collection of The
Cleveland Museum of Art, 1960.115

29

Underground, 1951
Pastel and graphite
on paper, 18 x 11 7/8 in
(45.72 x 30.16 cm)
Private collection

30

The Flesh Eaters, 1952
Oil and charcoal on canvas, 60 x 72 1/8 in
(152.4 x 183.2 cm)
New York, The Metropolitan Museum
of Art, Purchase, George A. Hearn Fund,
Arthur Hoppock Hearn Fund, and Hearn
Funds. Bequest of Charles F. Iklé, and
Gifts of Mrs. Carroll J. Post and Mrs.
George S. Armory, by exchange, 1995
(1995.234)

31
Sleep, 1952
Oil on canvas, 24 x 30 in
(60.96 x 76.2 cm)
New Orleans Museum of Art.
Gift of Muriel Bultman Francis

90

34
Phantom, 1953
Oil on canvas, 30 x 38 in
(76.2 x 96.52 cm)
Dr. Joseph Cunningham and Dr. Bruce
Barnes

94

35
Primeval Landscape, 1953
Oil on canvas, 60 x 72 in
(152.4 x 182.88 cm)
Collection Elliot K. Wolk

36

Untitled (Study for Moby Dick), 1953–54
Graphite and pastel
on paper, 19 x 24 1/2 in
(48.26 x 62.23 cm)
Paul Francis and Titia Hulst

37

Flame, 1954
Oil on canvas, 47 7/8 x 36 in
(121.60 x 91.44 cm)
The Helman Collection

96

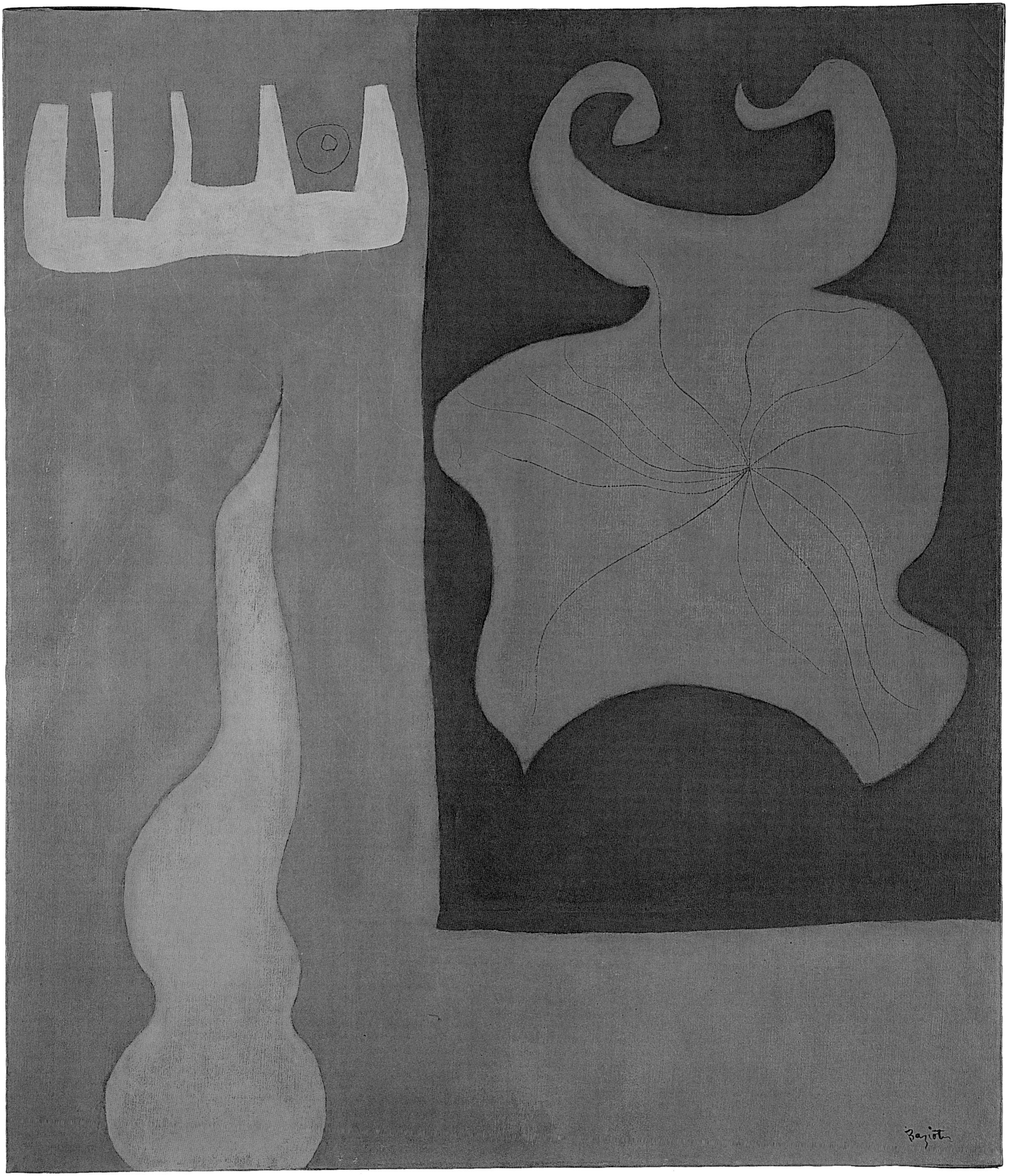

38

Black Night, 1954
Oil on canvas, 36 x 48 in
(91.44 x 121.92 cm)
Pittsburgh, Carnegie Museum
of Art, Patrons Art Fund.
Gift of Mr. and Mrs. James H. Beal, 1955

98

39
Moby Dick, 1955
Oil on canvas, 60 x 72 in
(152.4 x 178 cm)
Private collection

Page 100
40
The Pond, 1955
Oil and pencil on canvas, 72 x 66 in
(182.88 x 167.64 cm)
The Detroit Institute of Arts, Founders
Society Purchase, Friends of Modern
Art Fund

Page 101
41
Red Landscape, 1956
Oil on canvas, 72 1/4 x 60 1/4 in
(183.52 x 153.04 cm)
The Minneapolis Institute of Arts,
The Julia B. Bigelow Fund

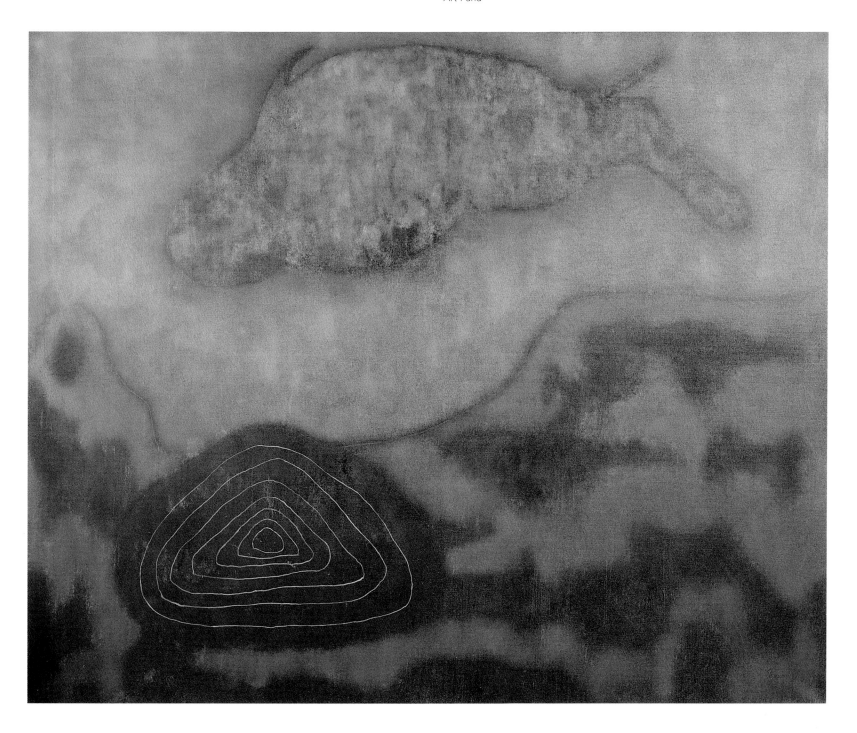

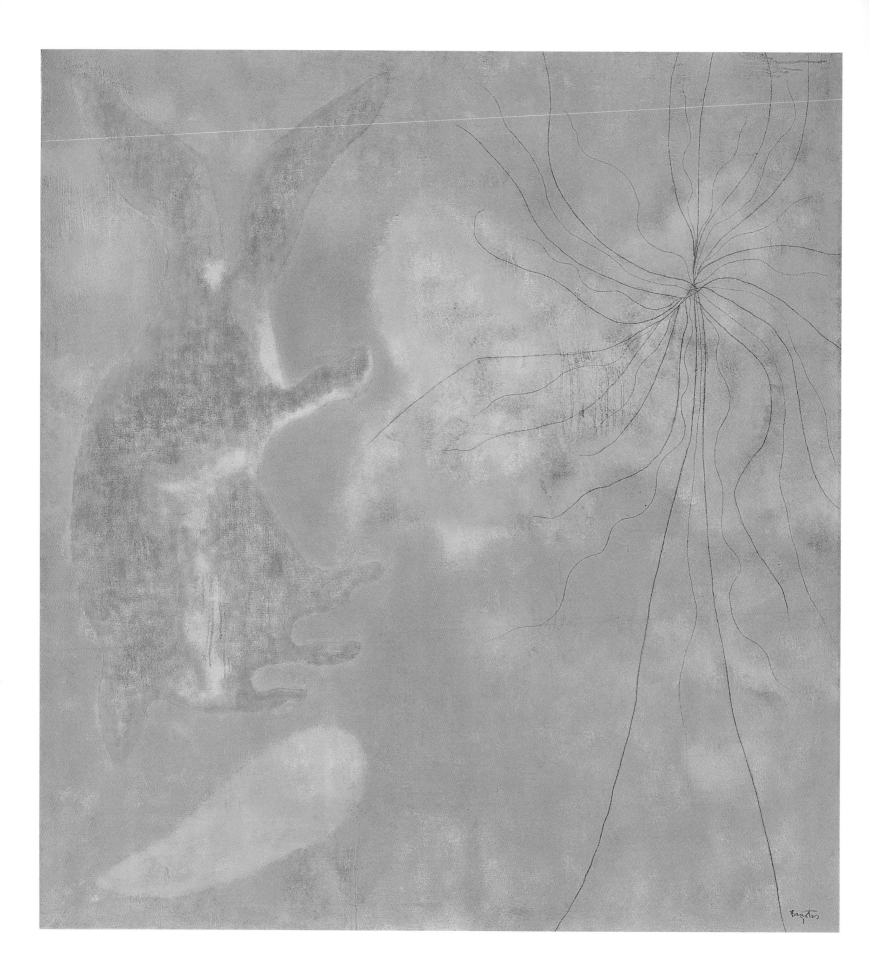

42
Spider, 1956
Oil on canvas, 14 1/4 x 18 in
(36.20 x 45.72 cm)
Courtesy Michael Rosenfeld Gallery,
New York

102

43

Cobra, 1957
Watercolor and pencil
on paper, 18 3/8 x 24 1/4 in
(46.7 x 61.6 cm)
New York, The Metropolitan Museum
of Art. Anonymous Gift, in honor
of Tullio Lombardo, 1972

44
Sand, 1957
Oil on canvas, 48 x 36 in
(121.92 x 91.44 cm)
New York, Whitney Museum of
American Art, Lawrence H. Bloedel
Bequest

45
Green Night, 1957
Oil on canvas, 36 1/8 x 48 1/8 in
(91.76 x 122.24 cm)
Washington, D.C., Hirshhorn Museum
and Sculpture Garden, Smithsonian
Institution. Gift of the Joseph H.
Hirshhorn Foundation, 1966

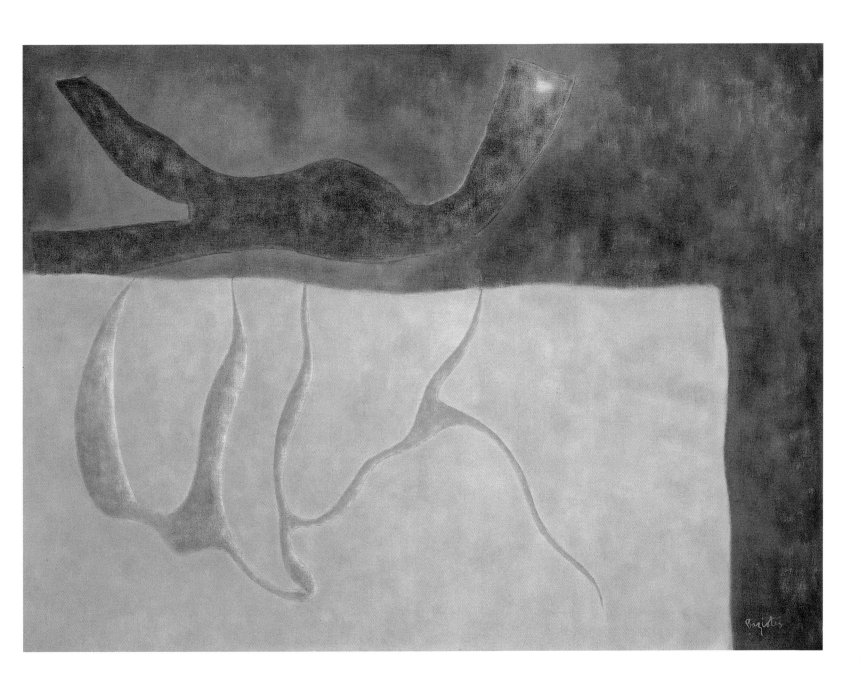

46
Prehistoric, 1957
Watercolor and graphite
on paper, 23 1/2 x 17 5/8 in
(59.69 x 44.77 cm)
Private collection

106

47
Watercolor # 2, circa 1958
Watercolor with pencil
on paper, 14 13/16 x 19 3/4 in
(37.62 x 50.17 cm)
Washington, D.C., Hirshhorn Museum
and Sculpture Garden, Smithsonian
Institution. Gift of the Joseph
H. Hirshhorn Foundation, 1966

48
Watercolor # 3 (recto)
Cancelled Watercolor (*verso*), circa 1958
Watercolor and pencil on paper (*recto*);
watercolor and pen and ink on paper
(*verso*), 14 3/4 x 19 3/4 in
(37.47 x 50.17 cm)
Washington, D.C., Hirshhorn Museum
and Sculpture Garden, Smithsonian
Institution. Gift of the Joseph
H. Hirshhorn Foundation, 1966

49
Dusk, 1958
Oil on canvas, 60 3/8 x 48 1/4 in
(153.3 x 122.5 cm)
New York, Solomon R. Guggenheim
Museum

108

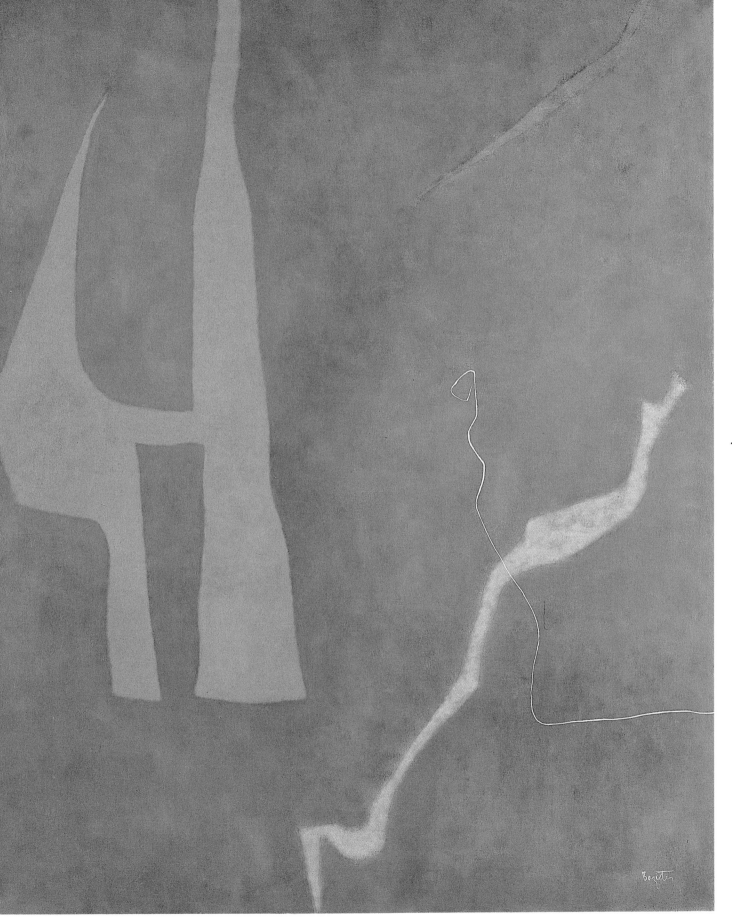

50

Iridescent Forms, 1958
Watercolor and graphite on textured
wove paper, 14 3/4 x 17 1/2 in
(37.47 x 44.45 cm)
Washington, D.C., National Gallery
of Art. Gift of Ethel Baziotes in honor
of Adlai E. Stevenson and Chief Joseph
of the Nez Perce 2004

110

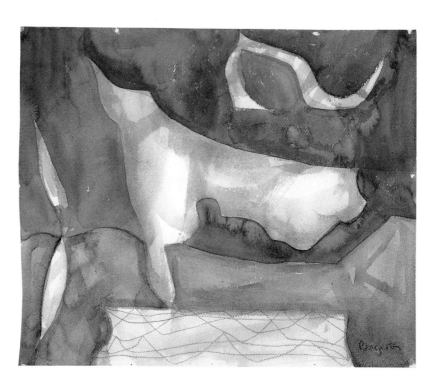

51

Flesh Form and Web, 1959
Watercolor and pencil
on paper, 17 7/8 x 22 3/4 in
(45.4 x 57.7 cm)
New York, Solomon R. Guggenheim
Museum. Anonymous gift, in memory
of the beautiful and tormented Gericault,
1972

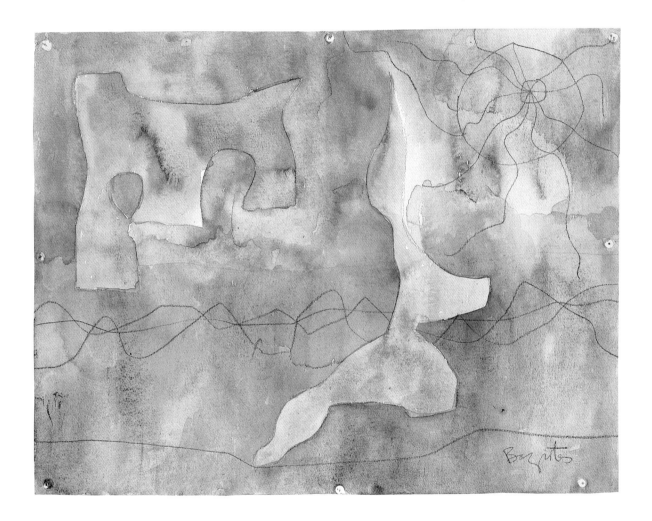

52

Reclining Forms in Autumn, 1959
Watercolor and graphite
on paper, 9 3/4 x 14 3/4 in
(24.77 x 37.47 cm)
Estate of William Baziotes

53

Autumn Leaf, 1959
Oil on canvas, 60 x 48 in
(153.2 x 122.2 cm)
New York, Richard L. Feigen & Co.

112

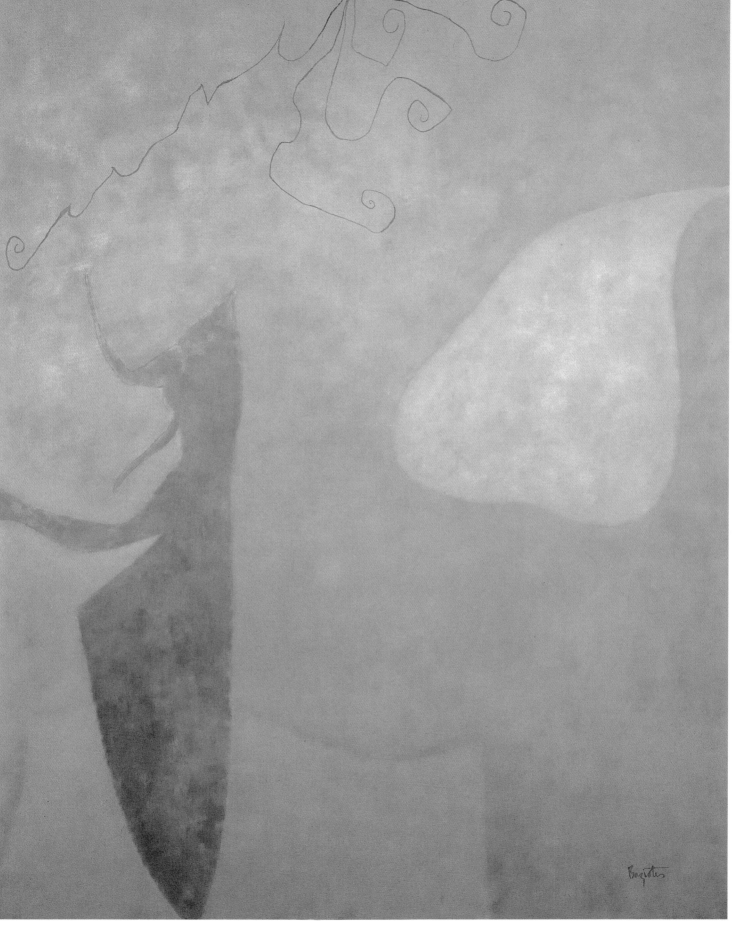

54

Scepter, 1960–61
Oil on canvas, 66 x 78 in
(167.64 x 198.12 cm)
Washington, D.C., Smithsonian
American Art Museum. Gift
of S.C. Johnson & Son, Inc.

55

Mariner, 1960–61
Oil on canvas, 66 x 68 in
(167.64 x 172.72 cm)
Austin, Jack S. Blanton Museum of Art,
The University of Texas at Austin.
Gift of Mari and James A. Michener, 1991

56
Aquatic, 1961
Oil on canvas , 66 x 78 1/8 in
(167.6 x 198.4 cm)
New York, Solomon R. Guggenheim
Museum. Collective anonymous gift, 1963

57
Untitled, 1962
Watercolor on paper, 17 x 14 in
(43.18 x 35.56 cm)
Estate of William Baziotes

William Baziotes: Chronology

Tatiana Cuevas Guevara

This chronology compiles information drawn from both published and unpublished literature on William Baziotes. Sources include: D. Paneth, William Baziotes: A Literary Portrait, *based on an interview from 1952 (unpublished manuscript), William and Ethel Baziotes Papers, 1916-1992, Archives of American Art, Smithsonian Institution, Washington, D.C.; M.P. Lader,* Peggy Guggenheim Art of This Century: The Surrealist Milieu and the American Avant-Garde, 1942-1947, *Ph.D. Art History Dissertation (University of Delaware, Newark, June 1981); and L. Alloway (ed.),* William Baziotes: A Memorial Exhibition, *exhibition catalogue (Solomon R. Guggenheim Museum, New York, 5 February–21 March 1965), New York, The Solomon R. Guggenheim Foundation, 1965.[1] When an event cannot be dated precisely within a given year, it appears at the beginning of that year. When known, titles, dates and current locations of works included in exhibitions are listed. Those works included in the present exhibition are indicated with their catalogue number in parentheses; others illustrated in this catalogue are noted accordingly. Only a selection of group shows is included.*

1912

11 June: Vasillios Angelus (William) Baziotes is born in Pittsburgh, Pennsylvania. His father, Frank Angelus Baziotes, emigrated from Greece to the United States in 1896 at the age of eleven. Having begun work as an ice cream peddler, he opened a lunchroom in downtown Pittsburgh in 1908. Three years later, he returned to his home village in Greece to find a wife. Following an introduction to Stella Eliopoulos, the daughter of a cheese vendor in the next village, they marry and return to live in Pittsburgh.

1913

Before William is a year old, the Baziotes family moves to Reading, Pennsylvania. A sister, Constance, and two brothers, Harry and Christos, are born. His father opens a restaurant, The Crystal, whose success enables the family to live in comfort in a seventeen-room house across from City Park, one of the prosperous parts of the city. William receives a privileged education at prestigious schools, without, however, any emphasis on music or art. The family spends the summers at Carsonia Park Lake and the nearby mountains.

1919

27 November: On Thanksgiving Day a fire devastates his father's restaurant, drastically affecting the family's financial situation. They are obliged to move to a two-room apartment adjacent to Reading's rail station, a run-down neighborhood lined with bars, brothels and dollar stores. His father opens a lunchroom and manages to sustain the family. William's schoolwork begins to fall off, he makes his first sketches, primarily caricatures.

1925–28

Having opened a bakery in 1921, the family gradually recovers economic stability and moves back to an apartment near City Park. Frank Baziotes begins to suffer poor health and a series of stress-related illnesses. William, now thirteen years old, experiences difficulty in re-establishing friendships in his old neighborhood. He is enrolled at the Elm and Madison School, but continues to show no academic interest. He contributes sketches to the 1925 school yearbook, leading to an invitation to join a drawing class. He accepts, motivated in part by his release from less

interesting classes. He subsequently drops the class, unwilling to respond to his teacher's call for greater commitment. He will not draw again for several years. On account of his constant absences, William is suspended during his sophomore year of high school. He finds work as an office boy in the advertising department of the *Reading Times,* where he will stay for close to two years. Having taken up boxing at the YMCA on South Seventh Street, he begins to train almost nightly. His mentor, Bobby "Bull" Ruttenberg, offers to train him as a professional.

1931–33

Baziotes works at the J. M. Kase & Company in Reading, a factory specializing in stained glass. He runs errands, learns to antique glass, and meets local artists working at the factory while studying at the Pennsylvania Academy of Fine Arts. With them he attends evening sketch classes, and develops an interest in Post-Impressionism and Cubism. He reads novels by American and European writers such as Thomas Mann and Jacob Wassermann, and befriends a local poet, Byron Vazakas, who introduces him to French symbolist poets such as Rimbaud, Mallarmé, Valéry and Verlaine. Vazakas gives him a copy of Charles Baudelaire's *Intimate Papers.* Its influence will be keenly felt throughout his artistic career. His father moves to Philadelphia to manage a cafeteria. Stella and the children remain in Reading.

Winter 1931: Baziotes visits New York for the first time to see the retrospective exhibition of Henri Matisse (3 November–6 December), organized by Alfred H. Barr, Jr., at The Museum of Modern Art (MoMA).

1933

August: Determined to pursue a career in the arts, Baziotes leaves Reading and moves to New York. The city is slowly recovering from the Depression. "The general atmosphere was awful [...] a continuous wave of poverty. Coffee lines. Riots. I doubled up with a relative who had a room on Fourteenth Street." Unable to afford the $25 a month fee requested by the Art Students League, he applies instead to the National Academy of Design without charge.

Fall: Baziotes begins studying painting at the Academy under Leon Kroll, attending class each morning and spending his afternoons visiting galleries. He takes a part-time job paid $8 a week re-setting pins in a bowling alley, but becomes ill through exhaustion and quits. His brother and sister begin to send him money to allow him to live and concentrate on his studies. He takes anatomy courses and begins copying from Old Master paintings and sculptures that he sees at the Metropolitan Museum of Art; criticism of his drawing ability from a teacher increases his determination.

1934

April: At the end of term, Baziotes returns to Reading for the summer. He converts his bedroom into a studio and sets himself a program of disciplined self-education: mornings are spent copying drawings, afternoons landscapes. He spends most evenings at a local beer garden. By the time the Fall term begins at the Academy in October, his draftsmanship has greatly improved.

1936

21 January–1 February: Baziotes exhibits his work for the first time in the "Second Exhibition," a group show at the Municipal Art Galleries, New York.

2 March–19 April: "Cubism and Abstract Art" is shown at MoMA, the first in a series of exhibitions organized between 1936–43 dedicated to the principal movements in modern art. The second, "Fantastic Art, Dada, Surrealism," opened later that year (7 December 1936–17 January 1937).

Spring–fall: Baziotes graduates from the National Academy of Design and

immediately finds employment under the Works Progress Administration (WPA, later renamed Work Projects Administration), a government relief agency established by President Franklin D. Roosevelt in 1935 to fund the building and improvement of America's infrastructure, arts, history, and culture. He is paid $23.86 a week as a teacher at the Queens Children's Museum, where his hours — three hours a day, five days a week — remain unchanged until 1938. He continues to paint every morning, while consciously eschewing the company of critics, curators and other artists.

1938

Baziotes is transferred to the WPA's Easel Division. He receives a stipend, in return for which he must produce at least four paintings a year. He begins to suffer from depression, however, and is unable to work for several months. When he is able to resume painting, his iconography of clowns and nudes, filtered through a personal interpretation of both Cubism and Surrealism, becomes increasingly dark and disturbed.

1939

Baziotes is invited by Kurt Seligmann, recently arrived in New York from France, to show a series of gouaches in a group exhibition. He declines, citing a need to overcome what he feels to be the overt influence of more established artists. Shortly afterwards, Baziotes meets Francis Lee, a photographer and filmmaker also employed by the WPA. The parties held at Lee's 10th Street loft, many of which Baziotes would subsequently attend, became a meeting place both for American artists and the Surrealist émigrés who arrived in the city in the late 1930s. It was here that Baziotes met numerous artists and collectors including Peter Busa, Jimmy Ernst, Gerome Kamrowski, Herbert Matter, Gordon Onslow Ford, and Jackson Pollock. The majority, like him, were employed by the WPA, and frequently worked alongside each other. Baziotes later recollected the excitement of the time: "... the talk was mostly of ideas in painting. There was an unconscious collaboration between artists. Whether you agreed or disagreed was of no consequence. It was exciting and you were compelled to paint over your head [...] If your

1

William Baziotes as a child in a formal portrait with his family, circa 1918 painting was criticized adversely, you either imitated someone to give it importance, or you simply suffered and painted harder to make your feelings on canvas convincing […] What does happen when artists meet is that we are able to see more clearly the unfolding of character as time goes on."[2]

Winter: Baziotes visits the exhibition "Picasso: Forty Years of His Art" at MoMA (15 November 1939– 7 January 1940). It would have a profound influence on his approach to painting. "Finally," he later recalled, "in front of one picture — a bone figure on a beach — I got it. I saw that the figure was not his real subject. The plasticity wasn't either — although the plasticity was great. No. Picasso had uncovered a feverishness in himself and is painting it — a feverishness of death and beauty."[3]

1940

Spring: While walking near 8th Street in Greenwich Village sometime before March, Baziotes meets a friend who introduces him to his future wife, Ethel Copstein. A native New Yorker, Ethel had attended Hunter College for two years, studying sociology.[4]

May: Baziotes meets Roberto Matta, who had arrived in New York in October 1939, at Lee's apartment. During this period Baziotes actively collaborates with other artists from the WPA, and makes his first forays into abstraction.

Spring: In the company of Pollock, Baziotes visits the exhibition "Joan Miró: Early Paintings" at the Pierre Matisse Gallery (March), and Wolfgang Paalen's show at the Julien Levy Gallery (9–22 April). Having explored Surrealist techniques since 1938, Baziotes encourages Pollock's own involvement with the movement.[5]

Winter 1940–41: Baziotes and Pollock meet at Kamrowski's studio and begin to discuss and experiment with automatist techniques. Improvizing on a canvas stretched out on the floor, the three artists brush and drip fast-drying lacquer to create the first in a series of collaborative works.

1941

22 January–8 March: Baziotes attends a series of lectures on Surrealism given by Onslow Ford at the New School of Social Research, New York. Others present include Jimmy Ernst, Frederick Kiesler, Matta, Pollock, Kay Sage,

Meyer Shapiro, and Yves Tanguy. Howard Putzel, a West Coast art dealer who had recently settled in New York following a stay in Europe, organizes a program of exhibitions to complement the lectures, including presentations of the work of Giorgio de Chirico, Max Ernst, René Magritte, Miró and Tanguy. The series concludes with an important group exhibition titled "Adventures in Surrealist Painting During the Last Four Years," featuring the work of Jean Arp, Victor Brauner, Paul Delvaux, Stanley William Hayter, André Masson, and Kurt Seligmann. Baziotes takes a particular interest in the section devoted to automatism, represented by the work of Matta, Onslow Ford and Paalen.

12 April: Baziotes marries Ethel Copstein, then twenty years old. They move between a series of apartments in the Upper West Side and Greenwich Village, before settling at 104th Street and Broadway.

14 July: Peggy Guggenheim arrives in New York, accompanied by her husband-to-be Max Ernst, and is reunited with her art collection.

Summer-fall: Jimmy Ernst becomes a frequent guest at the Baziotes' home. Baziotes assumes the role of an older brother to the younger artist and the two paint together at weekends. On one such Sunday (7 December 1941), Ernst hears the radio broadcast announcing the Japanese bombing of Pearl Harbor. He relays the news to Baziotes, who is next door in the final stages of the painting *The Accordion of Flesh* (circa 1941; cat. no. 5). "That's it," Ernst later recalled Baziotes saying, "Jesus Christ, that's it. We've got a war." According to Ernst, his mood and approach to the work immediately darkened, with a delicate line replaced by "a skein of electric impulses."[6]

December: Baziotes meets Robert Motherwell, recently returned from Mexico, at a dinner at Matta's apartment. They become close friends. Through Motherwell, Baziotes meets Peggy Guggenheim several months later.

Winter 1941–42: Visits MoMA to see the retrospective exhibition "Joan Miró" (19 November–11 January), organized by James Johnson Sweeney.

1942

February–March: Baziotes sees Masson's paintings at the artist's one-man show held jointly at the Willard

and Buchholz Galleries, New York (17 February–14 March).

Fall: Matta organizes a series of evening dinners in his apartment on 12th Street, during which several artists and their wives play Surrealist parlor games to produce automatist poems. Among the participants are William and Ethel Baziotes, Robert and Maria Motherwell, Lee Krasner and Jackson Pollock, Peter Busa and his future wife Jeanne Juell, and Matta and Ann Clark.

From October, the same group of artists, without wives, begins regularly to meet at Matta's studio on 9th Street on Saturday afternoons. Taking its lead from Matta's own experience of Surrealist collaborative work — he had spent the spring and summer of 1939 working with André Breton, Esteban Francés, Onslow Ford, and Tanguy at the Château Chemilliere, Brittany — the new group makes automatic drawings. After a handful of sessions, they disband following disagreements with Matta regarding their objectives.

14 October–7 November: At the invitation of couturier Elsa Schiaparelli, Breton organizes the exhibition "First Papers of Surrealism" at the Whitelaw Reid Mansion, 451 Madison Avenue, New York. Baziotes, one of a group of younger American artists including John Goodwin, David Hare, Kamrowski, Motherwell, Ralph Nelson, Barbara Reis, and Kay Sage invited by Breton to exhibit alongside the more established European exiles, shows *Leonardo da Vinci's Butterfly* (1942; cat. no. 6). The exhibition is spectacularly installed by Marcel Duchamp, who fills the galleries with his famous "mile of string."

20 October: Accompanied by Ethel, Baziotes attends the opening of Peggy Guggenheim's museum/gallery Art of This Century at 30 West 57th Street, New York. Designed by the Austrian architect Frederick Kiesler to display Peggy's collection of predominantly European modern art, it is also intended to be "a center where artists will be welcome and where they can feel that they are cooperating in establishing a research center for new ideas."[7]

December: Following the termination of the WPA, Baziotes, Busa, and Krasner enroll in a publicly-funded program designed to aid their transition to outside employment. Earning $17 per week, half of what

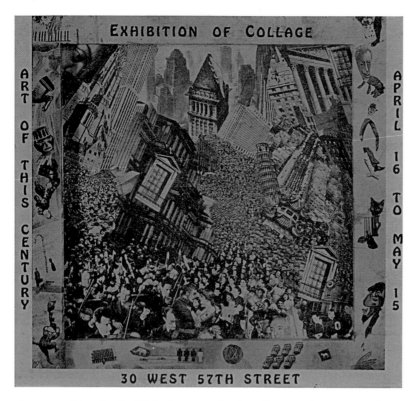

they were paid under the WPA, they find work in a mechanical drafting course at the New York Trade School on East 67th Street.

1943

February: Baziotes, Motherwell and Pollock are invited by Peggy Guggenheim to produce works for an exhibition of collage at her gallery.

15 March: Baziotes again exhibits *Leonardo da Vinci's Butterfly* (1942; cat. no. 6), this time in "Adventures in Perspective," the inaugural show at the Norlyst Gallery founded by Jimmy Ernst and Elenor Lust at 59 West 56th Street, New York. The exhibition includes works by some fifty artists, among them Milton Avery, Joseph Cornell, John Ferren, Adolph Gottlieb, Motherwell, Louise Nevelson, Mark Rothko, and Charles Seliger.

16 April–15 May: Baziotes exhibits *The Drugged Balloonist* (1943; cat. no. 9) in the "Exhibition of Collage" at Art of This Century, his first appearance at the gallery. Alongside works by renowned Europeans such as Arp, Duchamp, Max Ernst, Miró, Kurt Schwitters, and Picasso, hang collages, papiers collés and photomontages by younger New York-based artists including Jimmy Ernst, Hare, Kamrowski, Motherwell and Pollock.
The Drugged Balloonist (cat. no. 9) is purchased for $50

by the collector Saidie A. May and immediately donated to the Baltimore Museum of Art.

18 May–26 June: Baziotes is one of thirty-three artists under thirty-five years of age selected by a jury including Marcel Duchamp, Peggy Guggenheim, Piet Mondrian, Howard Putzel, James Thrall Soby, and James Johnson Sweeney to exhibit at the first "Spring Salon for Young Artists" at Art of This Century. He exhibits two works, *The Mirror at Midnight I* and *II* (circa 1942; cat. no. 7). Others chosen include Virginia Admiral, Busa, Kamrowski, Ibram Lassaw, Matta, Motherwell, I. Rice Pereira, Ad Reinhardt, Hedda Sterne, and Pollock (whose entry, *Stenographic Figure* [circa 1942, MoMA], Baziotes helped to select). Both paintings by Baziotes are sold from the exhibition for $150 each.[8]

July: At the same time that Pollock is awarded a contract by Art of This Century, Peggy Guggenheim and Putzel discuss the idea of formally representing Baziotes, and of organizing a first one-man exhibition of his work.[9] They visit his studio, § but find him depressed and unsettled. Baziotes decides to leave New York to spend the summer in Reading. Before he leaves Peggy Guggenheim, as a gesture of encouragement, purchases three gouaches and a small oil painting for $450. Among them is *Untitled*

(1943; cat. no. 10) which remains in her collection today.

Fall: Following an unproductive stay at home, Baziotes returns to New York. Peggy and Putzel again enquire as to his health, before deciding to postpone the exhibition to the following year.

9 November: Baziotes attends the opening of Jackson Pollock's début one-man show at Art of This Century (9–27 November).

December: A gallery advertisement for Art of This Century printed in *View* magazine includes the mention of a "First Exhibition of William Baziotes."[10]

1–31 December: Baziotes is included in the group show "Natural, Insane, Surrealist Art" at Art of This Century, most likely with a gouache or watercolor drawing. Among the European and American artists included are Alexander Calder, Cornell, Max Ernst, Paul Klee, Masson, Miró, Motherwell, Pollock and Tanguy.

1944

8 February–30 December: Baziotes exhibits *Opposing Mirrors* in the traveling exhibition "Abstract and Surrealist Art in the United States," organized by Sidney Janis and first presented at the Cincinnati Art Museum (8 February–12 March). It is subsequently shown at the Denver Art Museum, Seattle Art Museum, Santa Barbara Museum of Art and the San Francisco Museum of Art, before its final presentation at the Mortimer Brandt Gallery, New York (29 November–30 December) under the title "Abstract and Surrealist Art in America." The New York presentation coincides with the publication of Janis' anthology of the same name. At the request of the author, who had seen the work at Art of This Century, *The Balcony* (1944; fig. 5 in Michael Preble's essay in this catalogue) is reproduced, accompanied by a statement from the artist. "There is always a subject that is uppermost in my mind. Sometimes I am aware of it. Sometimes not. I keep working on my canvas until I think it is finished. The subject matter may be revealed to me in the middle of the work, or I may not recognize it until a long time afterward."[11]

9 May–3 June: Baziotes exhibits *The Balcony* (1944) in the second "Spring

Salon for Young Artists" at Art of This Century. The work, whose title is taken from a poem by Baudelaire, is the only painting of quality that the artist has been able to produce for several months. Twenty-four artists, including Hare, Jimmy Ernst, Perle Fine, Motherwell and Pollock, are selected for the exhibition, again by a jury.

Baziotes' depression and lack of productivity continue. His health suffers and he is advised by a doctor to rest and stop painting. Following a month in Reading, and two months in New York, his health improves.

Spring–summer: Peggy Guggenheim remains supportive, making a second purchase, primarily of works on paper, for $500.

Summer: Howard Putzel leaves Art of This Century to set up the 67 Gallery at 67 East 57th Street. The gallery opens in October the same year. Baziotes returns to Reading. Having stretched twenty-eight canvases, he begins painting on 15 July. By 15 August, all twenty-eight canvases are finished. He writes to both Clement Greenberg and Peggy Guggenheim with the news.

13 September: Peggy Guggenheim writes to Baziotes, offering him an October exhibition at Art of This Century.

3–21 October: "Paintings and Drawings by William Baziotes," the first one-man exhibition of the artist's work, is presented at Art of This Century. Installed by Baziotes with the help of Motherwell, it is the opening show of the gallery's third exhibition season. Twenty-four works, for sale between $25 and $200, are shown, including nineteen paintings, four gouaches, and the collage *The Drugged Balloonist* (cat. no. 9), lent by The Baltimore Museum of Art. The paintings include those previously shown in the gallery — *The Mirror at Midnight*[12] and *The Balcony* (1944) — along with new works produced during that summer such as *The Parachutists* (1944; cat. no. 15), *The Hourglass* (circa 1944; cat. no. 16), and *The Wine Glass* (1944; cat. no. 14). A press release, probably written by either Putzel or Sweeney, is issued shortly before the exhibition's opening. An announcement card is designed by Jimmy Ernst.

Six works are purchased directly from the exhibition: two are paintings,

including *The Boudoir* (1944; fig. 6 in Jasper Sharp's essay in this catalogue), purchased by the gallery's accountant Bernard Reis; four are gouaches, purchased by the gallery's new secretary Marius Bewley, the critic Milton Gendel, the collector Sam A. Lewisohn, and Maria Motherwell, wife of Robert. Other works from the exhibition were purchased following the exhibition's close by author and jazz critic Rudi Blesh,[13] future gallerist Leo Castelli, San Francisco curator Douglas McAgy, and Connecticut collector Lois Orswell. Baziotes, who had been nervous about the reception that his work would be accorded, is taken aback by the interest.

Clement Greenberg, who would himself later acquire a work from the show — *The Schoolroom* (1943; cat. no. 11) — describes Baziotes in *The Nation* as "unadulterated talent, natural painter and all painter. He issues in a single jet, deflected by nothing extraneous to painting. Two or three of his larger oils may become masterpieces in several years, once they stop disturbing us by their nervousness, by their unexampled colour — off-shades in the intervals between red and blue, red and yellow, yellow and green, all depth, involution, and glow — and by their very originality."[14]

24 October–11 November: Motherwell's début solo show, "Robert Motherwell 1944: Paintings, Papiers-collés, Drawings" is presented at Art of This Century. In his review for *The Nation*, Greenberg states that "the future of American painting depends on what [Motherwell], Baziotes, Pollock, and only a comparatively few others do from now on."[15]

November: *The Balcony* (1944) is reproduced in Wolfgang Paalen's *Dyn* maazine, as part of Robert Motherwell's article "Modern Painters World".[16]

4–30 December: Baziotes shows *The Room* in "Forty American Moderns" at Putzel's 67 Gallery.[17] Among the other artists included are Stuart Davis, Lyonel Feininger, Gottlieb, Hare, Hans Hofmann, Matta, Motherwell, Pereira, Pollock, Rothko, Seliger, David Smith, Rufino Tamayo, Dorothea Tanning, and Mark Tobey.

December: A gallery advertisement for Art of This Century appears in *View* magazine, promoting the gallery as "agents for Motherwell, Baziotes, David Hare…" It is the first time that Peggy Guggenheim publicly states her commitment to these artists.[18]

1945

26 January: Peggy sells *The Hourglass* (cat. no. 16), to Thomas B. Hess, the future editor of *Art News*, and writes to Baziotes with the good news. In the same letter she informs him that

George Wittenborn, the renowned New York art bookseller, has expressed interest in his work and wants to visit his studio.

Late January–early February: Motherwell writes to Baziotes to broach the idea of leaving Art of This Century for rival dealer Samuel Kootz, soon to open his own gallery.[19]

Mid–February: Kootz draws up a contract for Baziotes, offering him $200 a month in return for managing his work. Motherwell follows suit, having made his commitment conditional upon that of Baziotes. Baziotes will work with Samuel Kootz until 1958.

February: Baziotes exhibits *Three Doors* (cat. no. 12), lent by Peggy Guggenheim, in "Personal Statement: Painting Prophecy 1950" at The David Porter Gallery, Washington, D.C. It is one of the first exhibitions to attempt to define what would become known as Abstract Expressionism. Works by Arshile Gorky, Gottlieb, Willem de Kooning, Motherwell, Pollock, Rothko and Bradley Walker Tomlin, are also included. Baziotes' statement published in Sidney Janis' *Abstract and Surrealist Art in America* is reprinted in the catalogue. The exhibition later travels to several cities across the United States.

9 April: The Kootz Gallery opens at 15 East 57th Street, New York, with a mission to show both international artists and the leading protagonists of the American avant-garde.

May: Peggy Guggenheim sells three works by Baziotes, including *The Balcony* (1944), to the Santa Barbara collector and philanthropist Wright Ludington.[20]

6–30 October: Despite having signed contracts with Kootz, Baziotes and Motherwell are included in the "Autumn Salon" at Art of This Century. It would be the last occasion on which the two artists would show at the gallery. Among those making their first appearance at Art of This Century are Julien Beck, Ferren, Manny Farber, Gottlieb, Hayter, de Kooning, Robert De Niro, Seliger, and Clyfford Still.

1945–46

December–January: David Porter buys Baziotes' *Mannequin* from Samuel Kootz.

1946

12 February–2 March: "William Baziotes" is presented at the Kootz Gallery, the artist's second one-man exhibition. Twenty-four new paintings and watercolors are exhibited, among them *The Room* (1945; cat. no. 17) and *Still Life* (1945; cat. no. 18), which is purchased by Washington University in St. Louis. Other works exhibited include *Flower Head* (circa 1940s, Fred Jones Jr. Museum, The University of Oklahoma), *Wall Shadow, Green Form, Black and White, Statuette, Glass Form* and *Mirror Image*. The exhibition is extensively reviewed. With the exception of 1955 and 1957, Baziotes will have annual exhibitions at the Kootz Gallery until 1958, and is regularly included in the gallery's group shows.

5 February–13 March: Baziotes is included in the "Annual Exhibition of Contemporary American Sculpture, Watercolors, and Drawings" at the Whitney Museum. During the ten years that follow he is regularly invited to participate in the same exhibition.

1946–47

10 December–16 January: Baziotes is again selected to exhibit at the Whitney Museum, this time in the Painting Annual. He will participate each year until 1961, with just two exceptions.

1947

MoMA purchases *Dwarf* (1947; fig. 6 in Michael Preble's essay in this catalogue). The acquisition is reported in *Art Digest*.[21]

January: Baziotes is included alongside Romare Bearden, Byron Browne, Gottlieb, Carl Holty, and Motherwell in the group show "Introduction à la Peinture Moderne Américaine" at the Galerie Maeght, Paris. Samuel Kootz organizes the exhibition to demonstrate to the American public that the artists — all from his stable — have international standing. French critics express unanimous disapproval. "We are troubled to learn," writes Jean-José Marchand in *Combat* magazine, "that these painters are considered the bright hopes of the Samuel Kootz Gallery." Baziotes, however, is spared criticism. "Baziotes has much more talent and goes infinitely further in the direction of audacity."[22]

7–26 April: "William Baziotes," an exhibition of seventeen new paintings, is presented at the Kootz Gallery. Harold Rosenberg writes a commentary in the catalogue. Among the works exhibited are *Water Animal, Moon Forms* (1947), and *Night Landscape* (1947).

29 April–31 May: "First American Retrospective Exhibition of Theo van Doesburg, 1883-1931" is presented at Art of This Century. It is the last exhibition to be held at the gallery, following which Peggy Guggenheim leaves New York to return to Europe.

September: In a statement entitled "I Cannot Evolve Any Concrete Theory," published in the first issue of the periodical *Possibilities*, Baziotes describes his approach to painting. "I cannot evolve any concrete theory about painting. What happens on the canvas is unpredictable and surprising to me […] There is no particular system I follow when I begin a painting. Each painting has its own way of evolving. One may start with a few color areas on the canvas; another with a myriad of lines; and perhaps another with a profusion of colors. Each beginning suggests something. Once I sense the suggestion, I begin to paint intuitively. The suggestion then becomes a phantom that must be caught and made real. As I work, or when the painting is finished, the subject reveals itself […] I work on many canvases at once. In the morning I line them up against the wall of my studio. Some speak; some do not. They are mirrors. They tell me what I am like at the moment."[23]

1947–48

6 November–11 January: Baziotes exhibits *Cyclops* (1947; fig. 7 in Michael Preble's essay in this catalogue), in the "58th Annual Exhibition of Abstract and Surrealist Art" at the Art Institute of Chicago. The painting is acquired by the museum, and Baziotes is awarded the Walter M. Campana Memorial Purchase Prize of $1,000. He is the first of his generation of avant-garde American artists to receive official recognition. The award is roundly condemned by conservative critics, for whom Baziotes and his kind represent a certain decadence in American art. "The Rich-Campana prize," writes Peyton Boswell in *Art Digest*, "perhaps through compromise or default, went to *Cyclops* by William Baziotes, a picture bilious in color, sloppy in craftsmanship and ignorant in design."[24] However, Baziotes receives numerous letters of support acknowledging the importance of the award and purchase.

1948

Baziotes joins Hare, Motherwell, Barnett Newman, and Rothko to found and teach at the short-lived artist-run school of painting 'Subjects of the Artist' on East 8th Street, New York. The school holds regular Friday night lectures and panels before closing the following year.

The Museum of Non-Objective Painting, New York, purchases *Night Figure No. 1* (circa 1945; cat. no. 19).[25]

16 February–6 March: "Recent Paintings by William Baziotes" is presented at the Kootz Gallery. Samuel Kootz writes a commentary for the catalogue. Among the works shown is *Pierrot* (1947; cat. no. 21). In his review for *The New York Times*, Sam Hunter describes Baziotes' work as "among the most compelling and creative romantic abstract expressionism being done…"[26]

5 March: In response to the attacks on the American avant-garde that had followed Baziotes' award of the Walter M. Campana Memorial Purchase Prize the previous year, "The Modern Artist Speaks" forum is organized by a group of artists at MoMA.

25 May–11 July: Baziotes exhibits *Moon Forms* in "New Paintings to Know and Buy" at the Walker Art Center, Minneapolis.

6 June–15 September: Peggy Guggenheim is invited to present her collection at the XXIV Venice Biennale, in the vacant Greek pavilion. The exhibition, which marks the first exposure for many of the American artists to a European audience, is a great success and has a great impact on European artists and critics. Three works by Baziotes are included: *Three Doors* (cat. no. 12) and the gouaches *Untitled* (erroneously dated 1945 in the catalogue; cat. no. 10) and *The Room* (cat. no. 17).

Fall: Continuing an initiative that had begun with the 'Subjects of the Artist' school, Baziotes helps establish The Club on 8th Street, New York. It would quickly become a hub of activity for the New York School artists and remain so for the next decade.

4-5
William Baziotes in his West 104th Street apartment, photographed by Francis Lee, circa 1947

125

6
William Baziotes
at an easel, in his
West 104th Street
apartment,
photographed
by Francis Lee,
circa 1947

7
Exhibition
catalogue, XXIV
Biennale di
Venezia, 1948

8
Exhibition
catalogue, I Bienal
de São Paulo, 1951

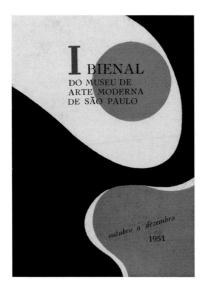

1949

For a period of three years beginning in 1949, Baziotes teaches painting every Saturday afternoon at the Brooklyn Museum Art School, and two evenings a week at New York University.

14 September–3 October: Baziotes exhibits *Sleepwalker* (undated, Museum of Contemporary Art, Chicago) in the landmark group show "The Intrasubjectives" at the Kootz Gallery. The exhibition, which brought together many of the artists and ideas that were later united under the term 'Abstract Expressionism,' was accompanied by a catalogue, text by Harold Rosenberg.

1950

Baziotes begins teaching at the People's Art Center, MoMA.
He participates in a three-day symposium at Studio 35, as part of the program moderated by Alfred J. Barr, Jr., intended to define the Abstract Expressionist movement. Other participants include James Brooks, Herbert Ferber, Hans Hofmann, de Kooning, Smith, Theodoros Stamos, and Walker Tomlin.

7–27 February: "New Paintings by Baziotes" is presented at the Kootz Gallery, New York. Thirteen works are shown, including *Dragon* (circa 1950, The Metropolitan Museum of Art), *Dying Bird* (1950, Neuberger Museum of Art, State University of New York), *Flight* and *Moonstruck*.

20 May: As part of the "Irascibles" group, Baziotes is one of twenty-eight artists to sign an open letter to the Metropolitan Museum of Art, New York, indicating a refusal to participate in a juried exhibition intended to increase the museum's collection of contemporary art. Fourteen of the signatories, Baziotes included, are photographed by Nina Leen for an article published the following year in *Life* magazine.

16 June–29 October: *Dragon* (circa 1950) is included in "100 American Painters of the 20th Century," an exhibition of works drawn from the collection of the Metropolitan Museum of Art.

3–31 December: Baziotes is included in "Current Trends in British and American Painting" at the Munson Williams Proctor Institute, Utica, New York.

1951

23 January–25 March: Baziotes exhibits *Blue Mirror* (1948) in "Abstract Painting and Sculpture in America" at MoMA.

12 February–5 March: "Lyrical New Paintings of William Baziotes" is presented at the Kootz Gallery.

4 March–15 April: Baziotes exhibits *Moon Animal* (1950; cat. no. 26) in "Contemporary American Painting" at The University of Illinois, Urbana. The work receives a purchase award during the University's Festival of Contemporary Art.

October–December: *The Somnambulist* (1951) is exhibited at the inaugural Bienal de São Paulo, Brazil.[27]

1951–52

26 December–5 January: Baziotes is included in "American Vanguard Art for Paris Exhibition" at Sidney Janis Gallery, New York.

1952

Baziotes is appointed Associate Professor of Art at Hunter College, New York, where he teaches painting from 1952 to 1962. The Whitney Museum purchases *Sea Forms* (1951; cat. no. 28). He provides a statement for Motherwell and Reinhardt's anthology *Modern Artists in America*. "Whereas certain people start with a recollection or an experience and paint that experience, to some of us the act of doing it becomes the experience; so that we are not quite clear why we are engaged on a particular work. And because we are more interested in plastic matters than we are in a matter of words, one can begin a picture and carry it through and stop it and do nothing about the title at all. All pictures are full of association."[28]

February–July: Baziotes is interviewed by Donald Paneth for *Commentary* magazine. At the request of the artist, the interview "William Baziotes: A Literary Portrait" is never published.

19 February–8 March: "William Baziotes" is presented at the Kootz Gallery. The exhibition includes *Primeval* (1952) and *Desert Landscape* (1951; cat. no. 27).

9 April–27 July: Baziotes is invited to participate in curator Dorothy C. Miller's exhibition "15 Americans" at MoMA. He is represented with eight works occupying a single room: *Dwarf* (1947), *Night Mirror* (1947; cat. no.

23), *Moon Forms* (1947), *Mummy* (1950, The Munson Williams Proctor Institute, Utica, New York), *Cat* (1950, Museum of Contemporary Art, Chicago), *Dragon* (circa 1950), *Toy World* (1951, Hollis Taggart Galleries, Chicago), and *Jungle* (1951). His 1947 statement "I Cannot Evolve Any Concrete Theory" is reprinted in the catalogue. Among the other artists included are Pollock, Rothko and Still.

1953

14 January–4 February: "Adolph Gottlieb, Robert Motherwell, William Baziotes, Hans Hofmann" is exhibited at the Arts Club of Chicago, following its presentation at the Paul Kantor Gallery, Los Angeles. Baziotes designs the announcement for the show. Among the eight works he exhibits is *Sleep* (1952; cat. no. 31).

16 February–14 March: "William Baziotes" is presented at the Kootz Gallery. *Grotto* (1952; cat. no. 32), and *Primeval Landscape* (1953; cat. no. 35), are among the works presented.

1953–54

13 December–February: Five works by Baziotes, one of which is *Night Mirror* (cat. no. 23), are included in the II Bienal de São Paulo.

1954

Three Doors (cat. no. 12) is one of thirty-six works donated by Peggy Guggenheim to the Tel Aviv Museum of Art.

23 February–13 March: "The 'Strange and Wonderful Fantasy' of William Baziotes" is presented at Kootz Gallery. Among the paintings and pastels shown are *Black Night* (1954; cat. no. 38), and *Dusk* (1958; cat. no. 49). Sydney Tillim discusses the artist's development in *Art Digest*. "His style has undergone consistently subtle refinement. He no longer depends on wispy radiance or the former mottled complexion of his surfaces. He paints better, crisper, more assured."[29]

12 May–25 July: *Flame* (1954; cat. no. 37), is included in "Younger American Painters" at the Solomon R. Guggenheim Museum, New York. Other exhibiting artists include Jimmy Ernst, Gottlieb, Philip Guston, Franz Kline, de Kooning, Alexander Liberman, Matta, Motherwell and Pollock.

23 May–2 July: Baziotes exhibits

Trance (1953) in "Reality and Fantasy 1900-1954" at the Walker Art Center, Minneapolis.

1955

The Carnegie Museum of Art, Pittsburgh, acquires *Black Night* (cat. no. 38).
Baziotes begins to spend more time in Reading. He rents an apartment at 219 South 16th Street and visits during the summers and for Easter and Christmas holidays. In a 1954 symposium he explained his need to escape the city. "I work regularly each day and keep fixed hours. I work well in the city and even better in the country — and by the country I mean a small city in America, with beautiful landscape nearby."[30] In so doing he gradually isolates himself from the New York artworld. Ethel Baziotes has recalled that her husband "spurned critics and dealers and even museum directors in order to avoid 'being caught in their web' of words and wrangling and inevitable compromise. The worst fate that could befall an artist, in Baziotes' estimation, was to become a 'phony' — an artist who abandoned 'his own kingdom' in a misguided search for acceptance and approval."[31]

April–May: Baziotes is included in "50 Ans d'Art aux États-Unis. Collections du Museum of Modern Art de New

York" at the Musée National d'Art Moderne, Paris.

11 May–7 August: Baziotes is included in "The New Decade" at the Whitney Museum. The exhibition travels to the San Francisco Museum of Art, the University of California at Los Angeles, Colorado Springs Fine Arts Center and the City Art Museum of St. Louis.

1956

5 January–12 February: Baziotes is included in the landmark exhibition "Modern Art in the United States" at the Tate Gallery, London. The works on display are drawn entirely from the collection of MoMA.

20 February–10 March: "William Baziotes" is presented at the Kootz Gallery. Among the works on show are *Moby Dick* (1955; cat. no. 39) and *Spider* (1956; cat. no. 42). Baziotes is interviewed for Hunter College's *Perspective* magazine. "My whole intention in painting is to make a thing poetical; but not poetical in a literary sense. I want something that evokes mood, a background, a stage set for certain characters that are playing certain parts. When I paint, I do not consider myself an abstractionist in the sense that I'm trying to create beautiful forms that fit together like a puzzle. The things in my painting are

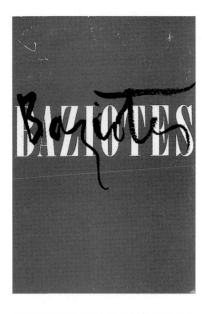

intended to strike something that is an emotional involvement — that has to do with the human personality and all the mysteries of life, not simply colors or abstract balances. To me, it's all reality."[32]

1957

24 January–17 February: Thirteen works by Baziotes, including *Primeval Landscape* (cat. no. 35), are presented in "The Magical Worlds of Redon, Klee, Baziotes" at the Contemporary Arts Museum, Houston, Texas.

1958

14 January–16 March: Baziotes shows *The Beach* (1955; fig. 13 in Michael Preble's essay in this catalogue) in the traveling exhibition "Nature in Abstraction." Opening at the Whitney Museum, the exhibition is subsequently presented in Washington, D.C., Fort Worth, Los Angeles, San Francisco, Minneapolis, and St. Louis. A statement by Baziotes is included in the catalogue. "In the beginning I drew and painted from nature in order to

know her. Then later, only to fall under her spell. And today, to let her mirror my thoughts and feelings."[33]
18 February–8 March: *Green Night* (1957; cat. no. 45) is among fourteen new works presented at the Kootz Gallery. Several days before the exhibition opens, the work is purchased by Joseph H. Hirshhorn.

1958–59

April–March: Baziotes exhibits *Dwarf* (1947), *Pompeii* (1955; fig. 14 in Michael Preble's essay in this catalogue), *Primeval Landscape* (cat. no. 35), and *Red Landscape* (1956; cat. no. 41) in "The New American Painting as Shown in Eight European Countries," a traveling exhibition organized by MoMA that is presented at museums in Basel, Milan, Madrid, Berlin, Amsterdam, Brussels, Paris, London. Baziotes' 1947 statement "I Cannot Evolve Any Concrete Theory" is reprinted in the catalogue.

1959

The Solomon R. Guggenheim Museum, New York, purchases *Dusk f* (cat. no. 49) from the Kootz Gallery. Baziotes leaves the Kootz Gallery for the Sidney Janis Gallery, New York.
24 January: Joseph H. Hirshhorn acquires a series of watercolors from the Kootz Gallery, including *Watercolor # 2* (circa 1958; cat. no. 47) and *Watercolor # 3* (circa 1958; cat. no. 48).
10 July–11 October: Baziotes exhibits three works — *Moon Forms* (1947), *Toy World* (1951), and *Morning* (1959) — in "Documenta II," Kassel, Germany.
Fall: "Notes on Painting," a statement by Baziotes, is published in the fourth issue of Philip Pavia's magazine *It Is*.[34]

1960 (figs. 12 e 13)

The Cleveland Museum of Art purchases *Water Form* (1947; cat. no. 24).
3 April–8 May: Baziotes shows *Green Night* (cat. no. 45) in the exhibition "60 American Painters: 1960" at the Walker Art Center, Minneapolis.

1961

6 January–5 February: *The Sea* (1959), is included in the "64th American Exhibition," at The Art Institute of Chicago. Baziotes is awarded the Frank Logan Medal.
13 March–8 April: "New Paintings

by Baziotes" is presented at the Sidney Janis Gallery.
8 April–7 May: Baziotes is included in "The Sidney Janis Painters," presented at The John and Mable Ringling Museum of Art, Sarasota, Florida. The catalogue reprints an extract from "Notes on Painting."

1962

Baziotes leaves the Sidney Janis Gallery. Following a brief relationship with the Saidenberg Gallery, New York, he joins the Marlborough Gallery, New York.
28 February–30 March: Baziotes is included in "Vanguard American Paintings," an exhibition organized by the Solomon R. Guggenheim Museum and presented in several European countries including Austria, Germany, Great Britain and the former Yugoslavia.
21 April–21 October: Baziotes is included in the exhibition "American Art Since 1950," presented in the Fine Arts Pavilion at the Seattle World's Fair.

1963

6 June: Baziotes dies from lung cancer at his home in New York, days before his 51st birthday.

1964

20 June–18 October: *Aquatic* (1961; cat. no. 56) is shown in the U.S. Pavilion at the XXXII Venice Biennale.

1965

5 February–21 March: Curated by Lawrence Alloway, "William Baziotes - A Memorial Exhibition" is presented at the Solomon R. Guggenheim Museum. "Baziotes is one of that generation of American painters," writes Alloway in the catalogue, "who changed their contemporaries' ideas about art and, at the same time, met inherited standards of traditional art, without appearing to, and without an ambition to do so."[35] The exhibition tours to Cincinnati, Reading, Santa Barbara, Milwaukee, Waltham (Massachusetts), Utica (New York), Columbus (Ohio), Washington, D.C., Minneapolis, Dallas, and Akron (Ohio).
The New York Times assessed his achievement: "If [Baziotes] lacked the brashness of abstract expressionism's more clamorous performers, he had a genuine sensuous gift that will assure

him a niche in the annals of American painting."[36]

1966
Seven works by Baziotes, including *Green Night* (cat. no. 45), *Watercolor # 2* (cat. no. 47) and *Watercolor # 3* (cat. no. 48), are donated to the Hirshhorn Museum and Sculpture Garden, Washington, D.C., by the Joseph H. Hirshhorn Foundation.[37]

1971
11 February–6 March: "William Baziotes: Late Work, 1946-1962" is presented at the Marlborough Gallery, 41 East 57th Street, New York. The press release announces the works on show as "the culmination of Baziotes' evolution."[38]

1978
24 March–10 December: The Newport Harbor Art Museum, Newport Beach, California, presents "William Baziotes: A Retrospective Exhibition," curated by Michael Preble.

1984
The National Gallery of Art in Washington, D.C. acquires *Pierrot* (cat. no. 21) through the Ailsa Mellon Bruce Fund.
7–31 March: "William Baziotes: Paintings and Works on Paper, 1952-1961" is presented at Blum Helman Gallery, 20 West 57th Street, New York.

1986–87
16 July–3 May: *Night Figure, No. 1* (cat. no. 19) is included in the traveling exhibition "The Interpretive Link: Abstract Surrealism Into Abstraction Expressionism, Works on Paper, 1938-1948," organized by the Newport Harbor Art Museum, Newport Beach, California.

1987
3 April–2 May: "William Baziotes: A Commemorative Exhibition" is presented at L. Feigen & Company, Chicago.

1995
18 January–4 March: "William Baziotes: 32 Years Later," is presented at Blum Helman Gallery.
January–24 February: "Baziotes, Kamrowski, Pollock: An Exhibition of Surrealism in the 1940's," is presented

at Washburn Gallery, New York. The exhibition includes works produced collaboratively in the winter of 1940–41 at Kamrowski's studio.
Fall: Having recently acquired *The Flesh Eaters* (1952; cat. no. 30), the Metropolitan Museum of Art includes it in the exhibition "Recent Acquisitions."

2000–01
19 November–7 January: "William Baziotes: The Poetic Spirit" is presented at The Butler Institute of American Art, Youngstown, Ohio. The exhibition presents works from 1938 to 1962.

[1] The author gratefully acknowledges the help of Ethel Baziotes, Michael Preble, Charles Seliger, and Jasper Sharp in observing the accuracy of this chronology, and the research assistance provided by Max Andrews, French Clements, Anna Drummond, Megan Fontanella, Ingrid Greenfield, Alexandra Greist, Ted Mann, and Jill Vetter.
[2] "Symposium: The Creative Process," in *Art Digest*, vol. 28, no. 8, 15 January 1954, p. 33.
[3] William Baziotes, in R. Blesh, *Modern Art U.S.A.*, New York, Alfred A. Knopf, 1956, pp. 268–69. Quoted by B. Cavaliere, "William Baziotes: The Subtlety of Life for the Artist," *William Baziotes: A Retrospective Exhibition*, Newport Harbor Art Museum, 1978, p. 36.
[4] Ethel described it as "love at first sight" in a conversation with Michael Preble, 28 June 2004. Baziotes, when interviewed by Donald Paneth in 1952, recalled the encounter to have happened at one of Francis Lee's parties.
[5] As related by S. Naifeh, G. White Smith, *Jackson Pollock. An American Saga*, London, Barrie&Jenkins, 1989, p. 416.
[6] J. Ernst, *A Not-So-Still Life*, New York, Puschcart Press, 1992, p. 219.
[7] Press release for Art of This Century, n.d. (circa 20 October 1942), New

York Public Library Pamphlet Box, Archives of American Art, Smithsonian Institution, Washington, D.C., microfilm N 429: 159–60.

[8] It is known that Rudi Blesh, the author, critic and connoisseur of jazz music, purchased two works from Art of This Century, including *The Mirror at Midnight I*, in 1945. Art of This Century's 1942 financial report lists *The Mirror at Midnight* (whether *I* or *II* is not known) as a handwritten addition to Peggy's own collection. Its absence from the 1945 financial report suggests it was sold. It is unclear whether this is the second version, or that acquired the same year by Blesh. J. Sharp, "Serving the Future - The Exhibitions at Art of This Century, 1942–47," *Peggy Guggenheim and Frederick Kiesler. The Story of Art of This Century*, edited by S. Davidson, P. Rylands, New York, The Solomon R. Guggenheim Foundation, 2004, pp. 309, 350.

[9] Peggy was interested in offering Baziotes a similar contract to the one she had given to Pollock, yet the financial situation of her gallery did not allow her.

[10] *View*, series III, no. 4, December 1943, inside cover.

[11] S. Janis, *Abstract and Surrealist Art in America*, New York, Reynal & Hitchcock, 1944, p. 101. This statement (with minor differences) also exists in typewritten form on Art of This Century letterhead (William and Ethel Baziotes Papers, 1916-1992, Archives of American Art, Smithsonian Institution, Washington, D.C., microfilm N 70-21: 47). It seems probable that it was originally written for this publication, yet it was possibly distributed to the press.

[12] It is unclear whether the work listed as *The Mirror at Midnight* was the first or second version. Both had been included in the 1943 Spring Salon.

[13] See footnote 8.

[14] C. Greenberg, "Art," *The Nation*, vol. 159, no. 20, 11 November 1944, p. 598.

[15] *Ibidem*, p. 599.

[16] R. Motherwell, "Modern Painters World," *Dyn 6*, edited by W. Paalen, Mexico, vol. 1, no. 6, November 1944, p. 61.

[17] It is believed that two works of the same title were produced by Baziotes within a year of each other. This work is not believed to be that purchased by Peggy Guggenheim early the following year.

[18] *View*, series IV, no. 4, December 1944, p. 109.

[19] "I told a man [Samuel Kootz] about you who might give you a contract if you want it — though I don't know how good the offer is. Anyhow, I spoke to Peggy about it, and she talks as though she is going to give up her gallery after this season, and as if it is up to us to fend for ourselves." Robert Motherwell to William Baziotes, undated correspondence, William and Ethel Baziotes Papers… cit., microfilm N 70-21: 141. According to Lader, the letter can be assigned a date of about January or early February 1945. M.P. Lader, *Peggy Guggenheim Art of This Century: The Surrealist Milieu and the American Avant-Garde, 1942-1947*, Ph.D. Art History Dissertation, University of Delaware, Newark, June 1981, p. 294.

[20] Observed by M.P. Lader, *op. cit.*, p. 269, in accordance with an undated correspondence from Robert Motherwell to William Baziotes (William and Ethel Baziotes Papers… cit.). Although the letter is undated, other references within it to an exhibition of works by Wolfgang Paalen at Art of This Century suggest a date of May 1945.

[21] "Baziotes acquired by Modern," *Art Digest*, vol. 22, no. 3, 1 November 1947, p. 26.

[22] J.-J. Marchand, "Introduction à l'art américain contemporain," *Combat*, 9 April 1947, p. 2.

[23] W. Baziotes, "I Cannot Evolve Any Concrete Theory," *Possibilities*, 1, New York, Wittenborn, Schultz Inc., no. 1, winter 1947–48, p. 2.

[24] P. Boswell, "Chicago Surveys the Abstract and Surrealist Art of America," *Art Digest*, vol. 22, no. 6, 15 November 1947.

[25] Opened in 1939 under the directorship of Hilla Rebay to display Solomon R. Guggenheim's massive collection of abstract European art, it was located at 24 East 54th Street, and in 1959 moved to its current site at Fifth Avenue and 89th Street, becoming the Solomon R. Guggenheim Museum.

[26] S. Hunter, "Baziotes," *The New York Times*, 22 February 1948.

[27] *Natureza morta-mascaras*, 1946, is the second work Baziotes presented at the 1951 Bienal de São Paulo. Its English title and current location were not possible to identify at the time of this publication.

[28] Excerpt from R. Motherwell, A. Reinhardt (eds.), *Modern Artists in America*, New York, Wittenborn, Schultz Inc., no. 1, 1952, pp. 11, 13–17, 19.

[29] S. Tillim, "57th Street: William Baziotes," *Art Digest*, vol. 29, no. 11, 1 March 1954, p. 17.

[30] "Symposium: The Creative Process" cit., p. 16.

[31] Interview with Ethel Baziotes, quoted in S. Naifeh, G. White Smith, *op. cit.*, p. 417.

[32] P. Franks, M. White (eds.), "An interview with William Baziotes," *Perspective No. 2*, Hunter College, New York, n.d. [1956–57], pp. 27, 29–30. Quoted by S. Tumarkin, A. Hildreth, "Statements by the Artist," L. Alloway (ed.), *William Baziotes. A Memorial Exhibition*, New York, The Solomon R. Guggenheim Foundation, 1965, p. 42.

[33] *Nature in Abstraction. The Relationship of Abstract Painting and Sculpture to Nature in Twentieth-Century American Art*, New York, The Whitney Museum of American Art-The Macmillan company, 1958, p. 61.

[34] New York, no. 4, autumn 1959, p. 11 – *Bulletin*, vol. 1, no. 3, 1961.

[35] L. Alloway, *op. cit.*.

[36] S. Preston, "Art: Three Guggenheim Exhibitions," *The New York Times*, 5 February 1965.

[37] Joseph H. Hirshhorn had acquired these three pieces from Samuel M. Kootz Gallery between 1958–59.

[38] Press release, "William Baziotes," Marlborough Gallery, February 1971.

Selected Bibliography

Statements by the Artist

1947–48
Baziotes, William, "I Cannot Evolve Any Concrete Theory," *Possibilities 1,* no. 1, Winter, 1947–48.

1948
Baziotes, William, Statement, *The Tiger's Eye,* I, no. 5, 20 October 1948.

1949
Baziotes, William, "The Artist and his Mirror," *Right Angle,* Washington, D.C., III, no. 2, June 1949.

1954
Baziotes, William, "Symposium: The Creative Process," *Art Digest,* XXVIII, no. 8, 15 January 1954.

1955
Baziotes, William, Statement, in *The New Decade – Thirty-five American Painters and Sculptors,* John I.H. Gaur, New York, ed. Whitney Museum of American Art, 1955.

1956
Blesh, Rudi, *Modern Art USA,* New York, Alfred A. Knopf, 1956.

1956–57
Franks, Paula and White, Marion (eds.), "An Interview with William Baziotes," *Perspective,* no. 2, 1956–57.

1957
Freed, E.K. and Sharp, E., *The Magical World of Redon, Klee and Baziotes,* Houston, Contemporary Arts Museum, 1957.

1959
Baziotes, William, "Notes on Painting," *It Is,* no. 4, autumn 1959.

Paneth, Donald, "Interview," unpublished manuscript William and

Ethel Baziotes Papers, 1916-1992, Archives of American Art (Smithsonian Institution, Washington, D.C.), Microfilm N70-21.

William and Ethel Baziotes Papers, 1916-1992, Archives of American Art (Smithsonian Institution, Washington, D.C.), Microfilms N70-21, 4984, 4985. (These papers include such significant items as Baziotes' correspondence with Alfred H. Barr, Jr., Director of the Museum of Modern Art; teaching notes from Hunter College; and numerous insightful letters and notations.)

Articles

1947-48
Rosenberg, Harold, "The Shapes in a Baziotes Canvas," *Possibilities 1,* no. 1, Winter, 1947-48.

1964
"William Baziotes, 1912-1963," *Location,* I, no. 2, summer 1964. Articles by David Hare and Thomas B. Hess.

1965
Alloway, Lawrence, "The Biomorphic Forties," *Artforum,* vol. 4, 1965.
Sandler, Irving, "Baziotes: Modern Mythologist," *Art News,* LXIII, no. 10, February 1965.

2002–03
Sogna, Kathy M., "The Roots of His Style: Baziotes in Reading," *Historical Review of Berks County,* winter 2002–03.

Books and Exhibition Catalogues

1944
Janis, Sidney, *Abstract and Surrealist Art in America,* New York, Reynal & Hitchcock, 1944.

William Baziotes, photographed by Peter A. Juley & Son, circa 1953

1946
Guggenheim, Peggy, *Out of This Century: Confessions of an Art Addict,* New York, The Dial Press, 1946.

1965
Alloway, Lawrence (ed.), *William Baziotes. A Memorial Exhibition,* New York, The Solomon R. Guggenheim Foundation, 1965.

1968
Rubin, William S., *Dada, Surrealism and their Heritage,* New York, The Museum of Modern Art, 1968.

1970
Sandler, Irving, *The Triumph of American Painting: A History of Abstract Expressionism,* New York, Harper & Row, Publishers, 1970.

1971
William Baziotes: Late Work, 1946-1962, New York, Marlborough Gallery, 1971.

1976
Wechsler, Jeffrey, *Surrealism and American Art 1931-1947,* New Brunswick, Ruters, The State University, 1976.

1978

Preble, Michael (ed.), *William Baziotes: A Retrospective Exhibition*, Newport Harbor, California, Newport Harbor Art Museum, 1978. (Includes: M. Preble, "Introduction: An Appreciation of the Art of William Baziotes;" B. Cavaliere, "William Baziotes: The Subtlety of Life for the Artist;" M. Hadler, "William Baziotes: Four Sources of Inspiration.")

1981

Hobbs, Robert Carleton and Levin, Gail. *Abstract Expressionism: The Formative Years*, Ithaca, New York, Cornell University Press, 1981. (Includes: R. Carleton Hobbs, "Early Abstract Expressionism: A Concern with the Unknown Within;" G. Levin, "Miró, Kandinsky and the Genesis of Abstract Expressionism.")

1984

Preble, Michael, "William Baziotes," *William Baziotes, Paintings and Works on Paper, 1952-1961*, New York, Blum Helman Gallery, 1984.

1986

Schimmel, Paul, *The Interpretive Link: Abstract Surrealism into Abstract Expressionism, Works on Paper, 1938-1948*, Newport Harbor, California, Newport Harbor Art Museum, 1986. (Includes: P. Schimmel, "Images of Metamorphosis;" D. Ashton, "Crisis and Perpetual Resolution;" L. Alloway, "The Biomorphic Forties;" M. Sawin, "The Cycloptic Eye, Pataphysics and the Possible: Transformations of Surrealism;" P. Leider, "Surrealist and Not Surrealist in the Art of Jackson Pollock and His Contemporaries;" R.C. Hobbs, "The Victorian Unconscious: Tonalist Sources for Abstract Expressionism;" M. McNickle, "American Responses to Surrealism: Barnett Newman.")

1987

Bross, Louise and Rubin, David, *William Baziotes: A Commemorative Exhibition*, Reading, Pennsylvania, Freedman Gallery, Albright College, 1987.

1992

Kingsley, April, *The Turning Point: The Abstract Expressionists and the Transformation of American Art*, New York, Simon & Schuster, 1992.

1999

Terenzio, Stephanie (ed.), *The Collected Writings of Robert Motherwell*, Berkeley and Los Angeles, California, University of Los Angeles Press, 1999.

2000

Cole, Robert Reed and Zona, Louis, *Baziotes: The Poetic Spirit*, Howland, Ohio, The Butler Institute of American Art, 2000.

2002

Pollock's America – Jackson Pollock in Venice – The Irascibles and the New York School, Milan, Skira editore, 2002. (Included in *Jackson Pollock in Venice*: G. Romanelli, "Jackson Pollock at the Museo Correr 1950;" B. Alfieri, "The Pollock Exhibition;" P. Rylands, "Jackson Pollock and Peggy Guggenheim;" A. Bonito Oliva, "Ecumenical 'Furor';" S. Hunter, "An American Master: Jackson Pollock, 1930-1949, Myth and Reality;" E.G. Landau, "Jackson Pollock: The Body and Nature;" K. Varnedoe, "Comet: Jackson Pollock's Life and Work;" W.S. Lieberman, "Pollock's Sketchbook at the Morgan Library;" F. Pivano, "The America of Jackson Pollock." Included in *The Irascibles and the New York School*: S. Hunter, "The Most Outrageous 'Irascibles': Ad Reinhardt and the Color-Field Painters;" E.G. Landau, "Jackson Pollock and Lee Krasner: The Erotics of Influence;" E.G. Landau, "Channeling Desire: Lee Krasner's Collages of the Early 1950s." Annexes include: "Jackson Pollock," ed. by L. Maeran; The "Irascibles," ed. by L. Maeran and G. Sanfo.)

**Peggy Guggenheim Collection
Institutional Patrons**

Intrapresæ Collezione Guggenheim

Peggy Guggenheim Collection Staff

Banca del Gottardo
Regione Veneto

Alitalia
Arclinea
Automotive Products Italia
Barbero 1891
Bisazza
Corriere della Sera
Fitt
Gruppo 3M Italia
Hangar Design Group
Hausbrandt
Leo Burnett
Listone Giordano
Nicoletti
Palladio Finanziaria
Rex Built-In
Rubelli
Salvatore Ferragamo
Swatch
Wella

Director
Philip Rylands

Director's Secretary
Valentina Furlan

Director's Assistant for Projects
Michela Sala

Curator
Fred Licht

Associate Curator
Luca Massimo Barbero

Officer for Membership and Special Events
Claudia Rech

*Coordinator for Individual Membership
and Special Events*
Martina Pizzul

Officer for External Affairs
Liesbeth Bollen

*Assistant for Membership, Special Events
and External Affairs*
Orsola Bertini Curri

Officer for Corporate Development
Alessandra Bonetti Rubelli

Chief Accountant
Laura Micolucci

Accountant
Gabriella Andreatta

Accounting Assistants
Cinzia Marchetti
Susanna Favarato

*Manager of Special Projects
and Publications*
Chiara Barbieri

*Information Technology and Technical
Coordinator*
Roger Zuccolo

*Chief Registrar and Exhibitions & Collections
Coordinator*
Jasper Sharp

Registrar
Sandra Divari

Art Handling and Technical Services
Siro de Boni

Education and Visitor Services
Elena Minarelli

Entrance Supervisor
Patrizia Martignon

Librarian
Gabrielle Lewin

Manager of Retail Operations
Roque Luna

Book Buyer
Roberta Chiarotto

Retail Administrator
Mattia Talli

Museum Shop Staff
Elena Reggiani
Francesca Pagliarulo
Elisa Haidbauer
Valentina Goattin
Michela Diprima

Security
Alessandro Claut
Daniele Regolini
Valerio Naidi
Paolo Ganz
Oliviero Scaramuzza
Roberto Bon